TAKING THE $ELL OUT OF SALES

OUT OF SALES

DISCOVER HOW YOU CAN OVERCOME THE FEAR OF SELLING

NATALIE KLUN

BALBOA.
PRESS
A DIVISION OF HAY HOUSE

Balboa Press books may be ordered through booksellers or by contacting:

Balboa Press
A Division of Hay House
1663 Liberty Drive
Bloomington, IN 47403
www.balboapress.com
1 (877) 407-4847

Because of the dynamic nature of the Internet, any web addresses or links contained in this book may have changed since publication and may no longer be valid. The views expressed in this work are solely those of the author and do not necessarily reflect the views of the publisher, and the publisher hereby disclaims any responsibility for them.

The author of this book does not dispense medical advice or prescribe the use of any technique as a form of treatment for physical, emotional, or medical problems without the advice of a physician, either directly or indirectly. The intent of the author is only to offer information of a general nature to help you in your quest for emotional and spiritual well-being. In the event you use any of the information in this book for yourself, which is your constitutional right, the author and the publisher assume no responsibility for your actions.

Any people depicted in stock imagery provided by Thinkstock are models, and such images are being used for illustrative purposes only.
Certain stock imagery © Thinkstock.

Printed in the United States of America.

ISBN: 978-1-4525-2102-2 (sc)
ISBN: 978-1-4525-2104-6 (hc)
ISBN: 978-1-4525-2103-9 (e)

Library of Congress Control Number: 2014915379

Balboa Press rev. date: 10/08/2014

To my family and friends who have supported me,
believed in me, encouraged me, and love me.

To all the teachers who have taught me along the way
through the journey of bringing this work to life.

To those who know they have a purpose in this world,
may this book bring you a piece of what you are
searching for while you are on your journey.

CONTENTS

Preface

I have dedicated myself to a mission to shine my light among my sales colleagues around the world. I am taking an opportunity through this book to share something that is profound and yet simple. As I reflected on many of my life experiences, it wasn't until recently that I discovered a powerful insight to lead with an intention of service in all I do. This new awareness has brought about tremendous changes in my world.

I have been in sales for almost twenty years. As I reflect back upon my time in this competitive industry, I realize that, during my diverse exposure to a multitude of sales processes, I have not actually enjoyed the selling aspect of sales as much as the service facet. It has always been a great thrill for me to utilize my knowledge and expertise to be of service to those in my community. It wasn't until recently that I finally realized the power of our intentions and applied that to my business model as the owner of my own real estate brokerage.

I have experienced the many ups and downs that are an inevitable part of being a salesperson. It's not uncommon in our industry to meet many money-motivated individuals. In fact, I am one myself. But I found that, in focusing my intentions on service versus "what's in it for me," my business increased tremendously. I realized I was in a state of receiving when I was giving what I had to offer. I firmly believe that you can take the selling out of sales and be tremendously successful. I have experienced it and been inspired to share this invaluable knowledge with those who have devoted their lives to this roller-coaster ride of sales.

Over the past two decades, I have gained experience in a large variety of commercial environments such as hotel sales, securities, financial planning, insurance, and estate planning services. And now today, I work in real estate sales and property management. I have gained a vast amount of expertise and can share valuable insight through personal examples of how to find the power within to shift one's awareness from "me" to "we."

I have lived firsthand the changes that can occur when you do what you do best with the intention to be of service. I believe we can all channel the direction of our thoughts, actions, intentions, and words to translate them into a highly successful career and life purpose. It is my desire to share what I have learned and continue to be of service to others seeking the same balance and clarity I have found.

The world is shifting into a higher consciousness. We are looking for more inspiration and purpose in all areas of our lives, including perhaps the oldest form of interaction, sales. It's important to update old or antiquated ideals in this vocation to keep pace with our own spiritual growth. We all have an opportunity to serve in our individual and unique ways, that is, to contribute to our world and the people in it. My purpose is to help lead in the transition required in an industry that no longer benefits from ego-based sales tactics to one that allows for balance and fulfillment for everyone involved and helps others bid farewell to the fear of selling forever.

INTRODUCTION

I've had the pleasure of working in the sales industry for almost twenty years. During this time, I've participated in countless training programs, all of which left me with the nagging sense that something was missing. I was told what to do, how to do it, and when to do it, but this aggressive menu of high pressure sales tactics left me feeling disconnected from my customer and frustrated by the sales experience. Through my many trials and tribulations in this industry, I discovered that a key ingredient is missing in all of the sales techniques being used in today's market.

In my view, the current model for business sales is flawed because it only focuses on material outcome. The energy behind this mentality is a recipe for failure because, to be truly successful, abundance needs to come in both material and emotional balance for both you and the client. Having a clear intention of service, utilizing the law of attraction, and implementing higher awareness techniques to open new doors can create this balance.

Taking the $ell out of Sales helps bridge the growing disconnect between the sales arena participants and their clients within this expanding industry. Instead of asking "How many sales can I make?" we should be asking "How may I serve?" This question will help you make a critical shift from an ego-based career in sales to a life calling filled with purpose and fulfillment. Instilling this type of positive energy into your work can only result in the natural development of a business and life that dreams are made of.

Every person on this planet has the ability to be on a path of purpose, happiness, and opportunity. In *Taking the $ell out of Sales*, I will be demonstrating that the key ingredient of a successful career in sales is to be of service to others. Being of service to others, without any attachment to the end result, allows us to be in a receiving state with the universe. To create this shift in our perspective, I like to stress the importance of looking through the "we" lenses instead of the "me" lenses.

Within each chapter of *Taking the $ell out of Sales*, I will be identifying central obstacles and challenges present in this industry, along with key ingredients that will pave the way for becoming a successful and a fulfilled salesperson. Chapter topics include service, purpose, passion, balance, self-love, confidence, rejection, sharing, allowing, and an action plan.

Within the above themes, I hope to provide valuable lessons that will allow you to look within and see a way to change your reactions to the various obstacles that many of us often stumble upon while on our journey to finding success.

Each chapter will close with an easy process for dealing with these everyday occurrences using my interactive "4 × 4 Method." This technique works by utilizing four concepts—challenge, clear, change, and create—and multiplying them by the factor of four powerful steps. Not only will this method engage you to become involved in the process of change, it will also provide a clear and easy template for magnetizing life-changing thoughts.

It will be a fun and easy way to clear out the old and bring in the new.

CHAPTER 1

It's Quite Simple ... It's Service

The best way to find yourself is to lose
yourself in the service of others.

—Mahatma Gandhi

Service is the essence of our purpose. Service is the opportunity to channel the universe and contribute to making the world a loving and better place. It's time to take a step back and reevaluate the intention behind what we do in the sales world and the opportunities we are overlooking by not leading with the intention of service.

Let's break down service into the following categories and tap into the process of converting our intentions to be of pure service:

- Intention
- Quality vs. Quantity
- Your Day Job (AKA Business)
- Community, Personal, and Universal

Intention

In the sales world, the foundation for our everyday activities is focused on being productive, increasing sales, expanding our client base, and growing the pipeline. Based on my observations and experience in the sales industry, I've determined that money is the driving factor for most individuals. Money is a good motivator, but in some cases, it can cause

1

people to do things against their better judgment. I have seen many colleagues fall in the name of money, and most do not recover. I'm not saying that money should never motivate someone. I find money to be a good source of motivation, but it hasn't been my only one. I believe one's intention behind achieving financial success is the important concept to look at here.

When you get up every day and get ready to go to work, are you excited about your daily activities, or do you have to drag yourself out the door and count the seconds on the clock until your hourly obligations are completed? What if I told you there is a way to find joy in your job? Do you think it would change your perception or possibly inspire you to seek out activities that would feed your soul? It all starts with your outlook on what you do and how you channel it to become something more than just a job. It starts with intention and the desire to make something bigger than ourselves.

Throughout the years, I often felt like I was out of my league (in over my head), and through those beliefs, I developed some insecurities in how I was supposed to conduct myself while on the clock. I don't know if it is a product of starting at a young age and allowing those around me to feed me with doubt of my abilities. Who knows? But it was there, and it was a challenge.

We all know that, once we get into our own head, we become our own worst enemy. I decided the best way to overcome these insecurities was to become informed, to learn from the best, and to soak in as much empowering knowledge as possible. I threw myself into attending training classes, reading how-to books, and searching for that magic pill that would put me on top of the world. In all the sales training classes I participated in, I asked the right questions, listened, and took notes. I did it all. I engulfed myself in what I found to be a pattern of the "what to do and what not to do" in sales.

One particular class stands out where we worked on getting comfortable with a concept in sales called "cold calling," that is, phone prospecting. In this class, we were picking random phone numbers from the phone book and calling people, hoping to find someone who wanted to buy what we were offering. My instructor was a short, bald man, the drill sergeant of sales. He lined us up in a small office setting with our noses in a phone book and a phone to call out on.

A most intense critic, he hovered around the room, monitoring our progress. The grand finale for the class was the opportunity to break a board with our bare hands. I guess it was to prove to us that we could do anything, make a cold call and break a board. I found a seat in the back of the room to watch my fellow trainees, one by one, break a board on their first or second try. It looked easy.

When it was my turn, I found it was much more difficult than it appeared. I kept hitting it and hitting it, and it wouldn't break. My hand was starting to swell, and our drill sergeant was not going to let me stop until I broke it. Finally, my hand went through, and I don't know if it was relief or embarrassment, but I started to cry in front of the entire class.

I consider this story as an example of how I put everything I had into learning what it would take to become a successful salesperson, including attempting to break a board with my bare hand and humiliating myself in front of a class of fellow cold callers. Looking back, I was really trying to find a way to overcome my insecurities. And as most of us do, I was looking outside of myself to find the change I felt I needed.

I continued to take courses, but no matter what I did to improve myself as a salesperson, I still felt that something wasn't right and I had a bigger purpose to fill. At the time, I didn't think being a salesperson would bring me to a place of purpose or fulfillment. Then I was introduced to a life-changing book called *The Secret*. This book discusses the law of attraction and the ways we can literally create our world by shifting our thoughts and focusing on what we do want versus what we don't want.

As with everything, I threw myself into it. I soaked it all in and became aware of how I interacted with myself. I hate to admit that it wasn't very pleasant, and I definitely wasn't easy on myself. This began the process of bringing out what felt right to me through all I learned throughout my sales career.

For a long time, I had the belief that, in order to do something that I considered meaningful or of value, I needed to have tools that weren't available to me, such as a large sum of money or reach of a public figure. Then I realized something. What if I were to change the intentions behind what I was doing every day? What if my day-to-day work life

3

was the beginning of a journey toward purpose and meaning? What if it was already right in front of me?

As I looked back at all the trials and tribulations I endured over the last twenty years, insecurities, and negative self-talk, I realized I needed to make some changes. Once I made those changes, the floodgates opened. My life started to take new form, and my business began to flourish. I started treating myself with love and kindness, and I could let go of the baggage that formed my insecurities. It was literally as simple as changing my mind-set. But old habits are hard to break, and they will come back to haunt us if we allow them to.

Over the last few years, I have been on a journey of finding my purpose and exploring it. To create and maintain my intentions, I consciously decided that my number-one mission with my business was to be of service. I redirected my knowledge, talents, and experience to find fulfillment. I offered my skills to be of service to my clients, colleagues, and community.

Every single one of us has the same abilities and opportunities to be uplifting, insightful, and of service. We don't have to wait for something bigger and better to come along. It is not an entity that will find us or one outside of us. It is an awareness of the intention of our thoughts that will bring us to what we seek. Once we have this awareness, one by one, we can all change the passion we have for our work, our lives, and the world.

Quality vs. Quantity

In sales, the basis of being successful is a numbers game. The more people you talk to, the more contacts you have, the more ads you run, and the more emails you send, the more selling opportunities you create. It's about bringing your trade to the awareness of the masses. People will know whom to contact when they are ready to buy what you have to sell. For example, I am in real estate sales, so when someone decides he or she is ready to buy or sell a home and I have been in constant contact with him or her, he or she doesn't hesitate to pick up the phone and call me.

Over the last ten years while working in real estate sales, I have found that some people believe that those of us in the real estate sales community don't work hard. The perception can be that we sit around and wait for the phone to ring or we get to walk through houses all day. It's very gratifying to finish working with a client when he or she says, "You know, I had no idea how hard real estate agents worked until now." Those clients have inspired me to implement quality into my work and not focus so much on the quantity.

The day I decided to let go of the pressure I had been experiencing by working in sales and devoted myself to simply be of service, I felt a huge sense of relief. The stress, anxiety, and internal and external competiveness lifted. There is an abundance of business and enough to go around. It takes too much time and energy to worry and focus on beating out any of my fellow competitors. I want my business to be an exceptional one that offers a quality service to those in my community.

Clients don't want to be just another notch on a contact sheet in order for you to meet your annual goals. I have to laugh about it now because I remember the days of driving to the office and mentally preparing myself to make those daily phone calls and meet my daily number of contacts in order to be on track for my annual goals. I became so focused on that process that I completely lost sight of what I was really supposed to be doing: that is, being of service.

Interestingly, when I stopped that daily ritual and I just put it out into the universe that I would lead with the intention of service, my business literally tripled that year. I wasn't following a magic numbers formula. I wasn't putting myself through misery by doing what felt unnatural to me. I was simply allowing my intention of service to lead the way. As I reflect back on this unintentional experiment that I conducted, I realized that the clients I was working with were energetically noticing my intentions.

The takeaway here is that we have the laws of the universe working with us. When you have this knowledge, you can begin to change your outcome by being aligned with service. I don't recommend disregarding structure and your goals, but let them be secondary to your intention of service. You will find that you become magnetic and your experiences, knowledge, and skills will be beneficial to those you are serving. You will experience a shift in quantity by offering quality.

Your Day Job (AKA Your Business)

Typically, we work for a local small company or medium to large corporation, and we don't consider the job we do to be our own business. We have managers, supervisors, or bosses who provide internal structures that separate different tasks into departments or divisions. We are just a small piece of the business puzzle. Companies have various operations happening simultaneously, but all operations typically have a common end result. Take a moment, and think about your own job and your contribution to the company you work for. If you decided not to show up for work tomorrow, how would that impact the operations within the company?

Now let's change the concept of working for someone else completely and theoretically turn it into your own personal business. An opportunity could be seized here. Many people have a dream of one day owning their own company, to invent that next big product that would change the world, or to be an entertainer, writer, fashion designer, supermodel, professional athlete, or cutting-edge doctor. Typically, it is a profession that we are currently not in. However, in our everyday life, we have an opportunity to approach our daily activities with a broader mind-set and receive that fulfillment of our dreams, not just a paycheck.

When you treat your job as your business, regardless of what that job may be, you become fully invested. You want nothing more than for it to succeed and have the possibility of taking it to the next level. Your mission statement is to be the best you can be in what you do every day, and with that statement, you become a person of service to those who surround you: your co-workers, clients, neighbors, community, family, and friends. Do you think you would have a little more pep in your step as you make your way to work with this change in the approach to your job? It's now your business, and your business needs you. You are the driving force. What sort of things do you think you will begin to attract by having a change in mind-set? Do you think you will gain more admiration or respect at work with your newfound love for your business? Do you think your clients will feel your shift in your new focus? Of course they will. It's no longer just a job; it's your business!

What does this have to do with service? We may not have the voice and dance moves of Beyonce or arm of Tom Brady, but what we do have is just as important. We have the ability to make an impact on everyone we encounter through our business. We have the ability to change the world, pay it forward, and inspire those we have the opportunity to be of service to. So now, your job is no longer a job. It has become a business, and your business has become a purpose.

Think about the effect that we can all have individually if we find our purpose in what we are already doing. We don't have to look outside of ourselves, become something we are not, and settle for not having a fulfilling life.

Personal, Community, and Universal

We have to believe in ourselves, and this mission starts with you. I can think of numerous times that I wanted to do something differently or try something new and I ended up talking myself out of it because I didn't think I was qualified. I am pretty sure I am not the only one who has passed on an opportunity because I was my own worst critic.

One night, a friend and I were driving home from a trip. We were just chatting as we drove, and I was asked a rather profound and unexpected question.

"Are you doing what you really want to be doing for a living? If you could choose, what would you really want to be doing?"

I thought about it for a minute. "Well, I have always wanted to be a writer. I would love to publish a book."

My answer surprised them, and they didn't know it was a dream of mine because I had tucked it way into a file that I labeled "You can't, so don't try!" I had never looked at what I was doing as a real estate sales agent as my dream job. I just did it because it seemed like a good career.

Then I asked the same question. The response I got struck me as quite sad.

"I just do what I do because it's what needs to get done. I don't know what I would be doing if I weren't doing what I do now."

I could be wrong, but my interpretation of that answer was that they were just settling. This conversation got me thinking. I decided I wasn't going to tuck away something that I really wanted to do. I surely wasn't going to just settle. I knew I needed to look within myself to find my purpose. I wanted to finally find what felt good to me and didn't feel forced or unnatural. This process brought me to the realization that I love to help people. I love to be an inspiration to someone. I love to be that person who makes someone else's day a little bit easier. I genuinely enjoy helping others.

I began to look at my work in real estate and saw how this was incorporated in my everyday activities. I was able to look around me and see that I could find love and gratification in my job and it didn't actually have anything to do with the process of selling.

This awareness blew me away. It didn't come from an external source that I was constantly seeking. It came from looking deeply into what I was truly doing versus just scanning the surface. This was so insightful to me and became the inspiration that brought me to the process of writing and doing what I have dreamt of doing. I couldn't have this life changing shift and not share it.

My next step was to dig a little deeper. If I could find this joy within myself, then I could benefit my community. And if I could help others see they have the same opportunity, we could go global and united we could have a universal effect on the world. It's a three-step process: personal, community, and universal.

You see that it starts within. Then we branch out into our communities, and as we all grow together, we begin to change the world. This concept is so simple. It's channeling something that doesn't require a costly education. We don't need tailored talents for this, and we certainly don't need to break a board with our hands! All we need is the ability to be of service, and literally, not one person in this world is not capable or does not possess this opportunity. It's quite simple. It's service!

Now, I would like to share with you a technique that is simple, fun, to the point, and, most importantly, empowering and uplifting. This process is called the 4 × 4 Method: Challenge, Clear, Change, and Create. It's a mouthful, and going forward, we will just refer to it as the 4 × 4 Method.

I wanted to take a moment and introduce you to this four-step process. Also, I want you to know how, by following this method, it will magnetize your thoughts as you process the old and bring in the new. Remember, your world is the product of your thoughts. If you don't like your world, simply change your thoughts.

Take a moment now to digest and think about what we have uncovered and then apply the 4 × 4 Method to cultivate a service mind-set.

4 × 4 Method

1. Identify your service opportunity. Ask yourself challenge questions:
   1. What does being of service mean to you?
   2. What situations make you feel you are being of service?
   3. What situations make you feel you are not being of service?
   4. How would you rate your intention of service on a scale from one to ten?

2. Identify the types of obstacles in your path to be working from a place of service. Please write four examples. This will help identify what needs to be cleared. For example, "I resent working with demanding clients."
   1.
   2.
   3.
   4.

3. Follow these steps to help clear obstacles for the ultimate service-based you! Here you are bringing about the change:
   1. Identify your earliest memory that formed your beliefs about work. For example, "You need to work hard for money" or "You need to find work that is fulfilling."
   2. If your beliefs are positive and service-based, praise your experience and honor them. Write it out. If you find your early experiences toward work are negative and ego-based, write down how you would have preferred it to be.

3. Visualize yourself within your positive scenarios, embracing that younger you and the wonderful experience of glorious purpose in your work through service.

4. Give thanks for the new awareness. Post a note where you will be able to see it to remind you regularly that abundant and fulfilling service-based intentions fill you!

4. State your goal/intention for creating the frequency of leading with service-based intention. Write the opposite to your list of obstacles here. Now it is time to create! For example, "I am grateful for the growth opportunities that always come with demanding clients."

1.

2.

3.

4.

CHAPTER 2

Finding Your Passion and Your Purpose

Passion is energy. Feel the power that comes
from focusing on what excites you.

—Oprah Winfrey

We want both passion and purpose in our lives. We want meaning. We want to feel energized and alive. And in this search, many of us focus on externals: if I change my job, if I take that course, and so forth. We compare ourselves to others who seem to have the dynamic and fulfilling lives we long for. But what if I were to tell you that you are already living a life of purpose and it's quite possible that your passion is patiently waiting for you? All it takes is a simple shift in the way you view your place in the world.

In this chapter, we will discuss passion and purpose, ways they relate to service, and ways we shift our intention behind the processes involved when working in sales. We begin this journey by looking within ourselves, rather than external circumstances, through the following concepts and ideas:

- Discover Passion
- Discover Purpose
- Stop Looking on the Outside
- No Makeover Necessary
- Back to the Basics

Discover Passion

We all had a childhood dream of what we wanted to be when we grew up. But as we mature into our young adult years, we tend to lose sight of those aspirations. I love to hear how children envision their adult lives. You typically will hear that they want to be a firefighter, police officer, teacher, doctor, or performer. Take a closer look. Can you identify the common trait? Most of those occupations are service-based. Children don't evaluate the occupation from the standpoint of how much money they will make and how it will enable them to make ends meet. Rather, they base their choices on what sounds fun or exciting.

At this tender age, it's all about passion and happiness. But as we enter our adult years, the values of our society have conditioned many of us, and we search for an occupation that will pay well, one that gives us the opportunity to be productive citizens and often requires an expensive education.

When I was a child, I wanted to be a number of things: an astronaut, fashion designer, and writer. The writer dream lingered, and I carried the desire and practices of writing by participating in writing classes and journalism through high school. I even began journalism school in my first year of college. But after starting my first sales job, I changed my major to business administration because it seemed like the most practical direction to go. Surely more opportunities would be made available to me. When I think back on my childhood and the dreams I held close during those years, I don't recall ever expressing any interest in a career in sales. Yet this is where I ended up.

I believe that, as children, our intuition leads us. Dreams of what we want to do when we grow up are not based on reasoning, but on an internal spark, one that always guides us to our passion. These passions have a way of coming full circle, demanding we honor them.

Take a moment, and think about what you wanted to do when you were a child. How does it compare to what you are doing today? Are you living that dream? If so, good job. But if not, how can you ignite that passion by evaluating the essence of your childhood desires and finding a way to bring that passion into your life today? Most of us don't end up in the occupation of our childhood dreams, but that doesn't mean the subconscious reasoning on why we wanted to be what we wanted to be can't come through in the here and now. Hold this awareness as I share more of my story with you.

I didn't grow up with a burning desire to fulfill a specific dream. I tried my fair share of different activities and sports, but either the chosen activity failed to hold my attention or I experienced a letdown and soon developed insecurities, which then led me to quit. But I had one thing that I enjoyed doing no matter what feedback I got, writing. I used to sit for hours writing short stories, songs, poems, and articles. It seemed to come so naturally to me. I became interested in writers such as Jim Morrison. Throughout the years, I kept a journal because I simply loved to write.

Now looking back, I didn't realize how strong this passion was within me. I just liked to do it, so I did it. How do we lose our passion for something that gives us such joy and a sense of purpose? Is it a product of growing up, becoming an adult, having responsibilities, and making sensible decisions? It's the only explanation I can offer.

I've spent hour upon hour working to make ends meet. I've spent years in an industry that offered me a lot of experiences, knowledge, and development of various skills, but it always left me feeling like something was missing. I never really felt passionate about being a salesperson, but I did it because it was a sound career, a doorway to starting a business and making an average living.

When I began to question my day job, I eventually discovered that the way to find lasting joy in my work as a salesperson was to lead with the intention of being of service to my staff, clients, and community. In discovering my new intention of leading with service only, I found myself face-to-face with my passion. My passion for writing snuck in through the backdoor and prompted me to share with the world that we all have the same opportunities to revert to our natural childhood instincts of leading with service. And we can find our opportunity to be of service through our business of sales.

Passion can come in many forms. For some, passion is music, art, running, sports, or teaching. And for others, passion is a career, business, or sales. Your passion is something that you can spend hours doing and yet it feels like only minutes have passed. It is that one thing you always want to be doing. How can you take that activity and channel it to incorporate a purpose? The beauty of it is that, no matter what you are doing, a passion will always lead you to purpose. It's just a matter of bringing forth the awareness and viewing it from a new perspective.

During an interview, Oprah was talking about her hair stylist who told her one-day that their passion was doing hair and their purpose was to make those they work on feel and look beautiful. It was beyond a job. It was beyond a passion. It was a purpose. We all share in this same opportunity to look at our day job in sales and begin to shift our perception of it as a job and lead with service to allow it to become a purpose.

The same goes for our passion. If you have discovered your passion—and it is an active part of your everyday life—then how can you change your perception of that passion to channel it into a purpose? The key is to ask yourself, "How does my passion serve others?" Whether it is your family, friends, neighbors, community, business, colleagues, or world, there is someone that your passion will serve. No longer is it solely for your own enjoyment.

Discover Purpose

Most of us are seeking a purpose, something that gives meaning to our day-to-day existence. I carried a belief for the longest time that my purpose was only to be obtained by changing who I was. I simply worked in sales. How could there be a purpose in that? Surely I had to transform, to become more outgoing and obtain more of an education. My purpose seemed veiled. It was a mystery I couldn't solve.

Truthfully, I was so busy looking outside of myself for my purpose that I didn't realize I was already experiencing it and living it. It was humbler than I thought it might be. It also brought me more peace and happiness than I'd imagined. I was to be of service. I couldn't believe the simplicity of it, and I let go of the need to change, to be bigger than who I was (more educated and/or an influential public figure), or to have the financial means to make a big difference in the world.

How do you go about examining your life to truly discover your purpose, and how does your passion tie in with this concept? The first step is to look inward as opposed to looking outside of yourself. It's human nature to depend on the aspects of the physical world to give us answers. The path to finding one's purpose begins by taking a deep look at what brings you joy and happiness, what fills you with enthusiasm, and what lights a fire within. Then you ask how you can apply that knowledge in discovering your purpose.

We have created a habit of just going about what we do in our daily lives without purpose. Once we are able to redirect our passion, become aware of our purpose, and see that it already exists in our everyday existence, we begin to experience fulfillment. We begin to take the ordinary and transform it into the extraordinary.

There are many great examples of people throughout history who have taken something ordinary and turned it into the extraordinary. I like to call them "game changers." They didn't just settle. They were bound to find their passion and purpose, and they then changed the views of the world.

Recently, I read *Onward* by Howard Schultz, the CEO of Starbucks. The story of Starbucks and the basis of this massive company intrigued me. In the early 1980s, Howard went to work for Starbucks, which was then only selling whole bean coffee or ground coffee, not actual beverages. After a trip to Milan, the European baristas, the elegant process of making an espresso, and the ways this was connecting people and creating a community among them inspired him.

Upon returning to the United States, he pitched the idea of bringing the romance of the European espresso to the United States and received an unfavorable response. He left Starbucks to open his own version of what he witnessed in Milan. In the late 1980s, he had an opportunity to buy Starbucks from the original owners. He scrambled to raise investor monies, and he was able to merge the two companies.

Howard's passion and purpose wasn't coffee. It was to inspire the human spirit. His philosophy was to start internally, take care of those who are working within the company, and create an environment that would change the way people would start their day. He led the company through many ups and downs. At times, he stepped down from CEO and returned when the company strayed away from the core foundation of the passion and purpose of its visionary.

One story in particular stood out. Howard decided to close all stores for one day to retrain the baristas on how to make the perfect espresso. The loss to the company was significant, amounting to around six million dollars, but it was important that Starbucks continued to offer the quality experience the customers expected and deserved.

It is fascinating to know a company like Starbucks started with a vision based on service, not only to their customers, but also to those who work for the company. Starbucks was the first company to offer benefits to part-time employees. Not only was this the foundation the company started with, it is the basis of what leads the company today. Whenever the company experienced downturns, along with every time the company grew to the next level, the key was always to go back to the vision of its creator. Starbuck's number-one priority is service. It isn't the bottom line or growth. By leading with the intention of service, it has become the company it is today.

In my own personal journey of discovering my purpose, I was taken back by the simplicity of it and, on the same level, the profoundness of it. As I began to change my intention behind what I was doing in my sales career to lead with purpose and the desire to be of service, I found that this was something we all share in common. Someone's purpose is not just exclusive to him or her individually. In fact, it's the opposite.

We share a common bond in living a shared purpose, which then enables us to reach far greater distances and more and more people. It's a multiplier effect. We all have our individual outlets, but the dynamics of the purpose doesn't change. In fact, it is shared. Once we bring this to our awareness, we can channel our passion and purpose through our individual outlets. This leads to personal enjoyment, fulfillment, change, and internal and external love. On a bigger scale, it gives all an opportunity to bring change to the world. Isn't that what living a purpose is really all about?

In the sales world, we all share in one common purpose with everyone we encounter on a daily basis. This purpose is to be of service. It doesn't matter if you work for a large company, you are an independent contractor, you are a small business owner, you are a retail clerk, or you are a real estate agent. I can go on and on because it applies to all. Leading with the intention of service gives us all the opportunity to be and do something bigger than who we are and what we do for a day job. It gives us a purpose.

The beauty of it is that we don't have to make any drastic changes to our worlds to begin to live this through. We simply need to change the intention behind what we do. Truly being of service will create new opportunities and sense of fulfillment and release challenges and feelings of competiveness because they can't exist when one is leading with service.

Stop Looking on the Outside

Probably the biggest challenge for me has been the concept that transformational change is not to be experienced by focusing on our externals. If you want to change the essence of who you are for the better or if you want to face your inner critic and move past those fears that keep you paralyzed, then you need to go within. This knowledge shifted my perspective on all that happens in my life, whether the experiences are pleasant or not. I discovered that being aware of my reaction to the unpleasant experiences in my life allowed me to grow in ways that I never anticipated.

Learning this lesson led me through the failure of a business; the loss of large business accounts, friends, and the foundation of a key relationship; health issues; and uncertainty of approaching an intersection in life with no clue as to which direction to take. It is the default reaction that we all have, and I am no exception. When we experience these life changers, we tend to place blame and look outside ourselves as to why this is happening to us. We develop insecurities, lose faith, form harsh opinions, and doubt ourselves.

In instances like this, when life throws us curveballs, a lesson is presenting itself. It is an opportunity to grow, dig deep, and decipher what the universe wants to reveal. These circumstances show up to teach us what we need to learn at that particular point in time, and they will continue to show up in various forms until the lesson is learned.

One lesson that has taken me quite some time to learn—and I came across many challenges on this journey—was the lesson to love myself unconditionally. This had been the core issue of mine, playing out in my relationships, health, and business. This newfound awareness allowed me to find peace in moments that used to unsettle me. I learned to look inward, silence the harsh internal critic, and communicate with myself in a more compassionate way.

Once I was able to identify the lesson of having genuine love for myself, my health improved almost immediately, my business continued to flourish, and I was able to finally let go and come to terms with a failed business that left a huge scar on my confidence, along with a significant financial loss. The love and care I needed was not to be found outside of myself. I had to find it within.

What circumstances are you experiencing that have you searching outside of yourself for the answers? Start to direct your search inward to see what you may discover.

The awakening I experienced when I finally got the lesson, that is, when I committed to journeying within for validation and love, left me feeling excited and inspired. No longer did I feel the pressure so common when working in a highly competitive industry. In my sales processes, I adopted the service intention, and everything I did simply became enjoyable. It's a win-win for those who I can be of service to and myself as I no longer felt that I was missing something in my work.

No Makeover Necessary

In society, we are taught to seek out perfection in all we do. We have many examples of what is considered perfection within the walls of our various cultures. The problem with perfection is that it does not actually exist. Perfection is based on individual perceptions. The search for perfection is like a dog chasing his own tail. We may feel we have achieved perfection to find someone who does not perceive perfection in the same manner. The pressure we put on ourselves to achieve something that does not exist is unrealistic. We are constantly searching for the quick fix, and when we don't find it, we experience self-pity and doubt our abilities. Then the search for perfection continues.

We live in a world of makeovers. We think we must become something that we are not in order to achieve the happiness we desire. But as we focus on what we do not want in our worlds, we end up creating more of it through the content of our thoughts. We don't want to gain weight, so we diet. We overdo it at the gym and weigh in daily, only to find that we continue to gain weight. It's a vicious and frustrating cycle. The key here is to stop focusing on the weight we don't want to gain. Instead, we can accept ourselves as we are, take care of ourselves with love and compassion, and let go of harsh restriction and self-loathing. By doing so, we begin to fall into our natural state of being, a place of acceptance and self-love.

This goes the same for our business life. I spent years focusing on what I didn't want to happen in my business to only experience one business failing and another just barely getting by. I kept looking for those fixes that would channel change and growth. Every day, I worked myself tirelessly. I developed stress-related health conditions and lived in a place of worry. I was unhappy. It literally took me changing my perception of what was happening around me to realize that, once I began to have more compassion toward myself and when I implemented the new service-based processes and let go of the pressure, all I didn't want in my world began to disappear. All I did want began to show up.

Back to the Basics

My journey in discovering my purpose and becoming reacquainted with my passion has led me back to the basics. When you are looking for something, you naturally begin to expect it to be hard to find. In *Love Yourself Like Your Life Depends On It*, Kamal Ravikant states that there is power in simplicity. I agree with that statement with all my being. That particular concept has revealed itself to me in profound ways that I never expected.

The core essence of who we are is love. But we believe it can't be that simple. It has to be more complex, we have to jazz it up, or we have to upgrade it. We live in a world of convenience, and the most amazing advancements surround us. So when it comes to ourselves, we don't realize that our transformation doesn't need to be cutting edge. It's really rediscovering the core basics. When you revert to this concept of love being your core essence, you begin to experience life in a whole new way.

You begin to look at those around you with compassion as we each go about our days, living out our individual journeys.

I have made it my mission to be a vessel of love to all I encounter because you never know when you will be face-to-face with someone who needs just what you have to offer in the moment. It doesn't have to be anything spectacular. It could be just a smile or kind exchange. It's become acceptable to not make contact with those we encounter in passing. We don't exchange a kind glance because we don't want to intrude. But a gesture like that has the potential to touch someone's heart … as well as our own.

When you discover your purpose is to be of service to those you encounter, you begin to seek any opportunity to be of service through your day job or exchanges in passing. It doesn't have to be complex. We have made it complex. It's really quite simple. Once again, we all share this opportunity. Embrace it, practice it, be kind to yourself and others, love yourself unconditionally, and love others. As you begin to embark on this journey of leading with service, you will find that happiness and joy come naturally. You become magnetic, and you begin to experience the abundance that the universe has to offer.

Take a moment now to digest and think about what we have uncovered. Then apply the 4 × 4 Method to find passion and purpose.

1. Identify your passion and purpose. Ask yourself challenge questions:
    1. What does living a passion and purpose mean to you?
    2. What situations make you feel you are living a passion and purpose?
    3. What situations make you feel you are not living a passion and purpose?
    4. How would you rate that you are living your passion and purpose on a scale from one to ten?

2. Identify the types of obstacles in your path to living your passion and purpose. Please write four examples. This will help identify what needs to be cleared. For example, "I have to make a substantial change in my life in order to live my passion and purpose."
    1.
    2.

3.

4.

3. Follow the steps to help clear obstacles for you to live your passion and purpose! Here you are bringing about the change:
    1. Identify your earliest memory that formed your passion and purpose. For example, "Not everyone is able to live with a passion and purpose."
    2. If your beliefs are positive in relation to living your passion and purpose, praise your experience, and honor them. Write it out. If you find your early experiences toward your passion and purpose are negative and ego-based, write how you would have preferred it to be.
    3. Visualize yourself within your positive scenarios, embracing that younger you and wonderful experience of living your passion and purpose.
    4. Give thanks for the new awareness. Post a note where you will be able to see it to remind you regularly that abundant and fulfilling passion and purpose-based intentions fill you!

4. State your goal/intention for creating the frequency of leading with your passion and purpose. Write the opposite to your list of obstacles here. Now it is time to create! For example, "I am grateful for the growth opportunities that allow me to live in my passion and purpose."
    1.
    2.
    3.
    4.

CHAPTER 3

Become the CEO of Your Life

If you're changing the world, you're working on important things. You're excited to get up in the morning.

—Larry Page, CEO of Google

For many of us, there simply is not enough time to accomplish everything that needs to be done. As the hours slip through our hands, we neglect certain areas of our lives in order to get through our looming to-do lists at the office and home and among family and friends. This vicious cycle can create undesirable outcomes. We feel more and more depleted as we watch our hopes and dreams drift further and further from our reach. It's time to look through our worldview lenses with a new perspective, from that of those who appear to have it all figured out, the successful CEOs of some of the most innovative and groundbreaking companies. It's time for us to take charge of our lives and begin to realize the hopes and dreams that will bring us happiness and fulfillment. As we've been exploring in chapter 2, this can be accomplished by truly finding joy in our day-to-day activities and living a purpose-filled life.

For a business to be successful, all the departments need to work together and support each other. In this chapter, I want you to think of your life as a business, one with the potential to be a thriving Fortune 500 company. We will look at ways to bring balance to all the departments of our lives through the following topics:

- The Role of a CEO
- Running Your Life as a Business

The Role of a CEO

What do Oprah Winfrey, Steve Jobs, Sam Walton, Mark Zuckerberg, and Jeff Bezos have in common? Aside from being CEOs of some of the most famous companies, they are visionaries who have had a significant impact on society and the world.

- Oprah Winfrey's vision brought divergent groups within our society together by engaging conversations through her talk show. She gave a voice to many, particularly women, and has empowered countless individuals.
- Steve Job's vision, via the viral use of Apple products, had a significant and far-reaching impact on our culture at large. He brought to life devices that changed the way we communicate, listen to music, and stay productive at home and work.
- Sam Walton's concepts changed the way the world purchased everyday necessities. The customer service philosophy that was a part of Sam Walton's vision created unparalleled customer loyalty and, in turn, created a massive company.
- Mark Zuckerberg's vision is changing the fabric of society and the way we interact with one another. Facebook has transformed our lives and become a part of our everyday processes, allowing us to share our unique voices, keep in touch with our friends and families, and build business through the power of his vision of social media.
- Jeff Bezos, the CEO of Amazon.com, created a web-based retail world, one that is ever evolving where consumers can get their needs met 24-7.

What they all have in common is a drive and vision. They built teams, trusted, went through highs and lows, persevered, and never let go of their dreams. They saw the end result before it was a reality. They evolved, they were optimistic, they thought outside of the box, and they didn't stop until they accomplished their goals, that is, until their dreams became realities. In their roles as CEOs, they accomplished a high level of success and broke barriers. They became trailblazers and brought to life visions that changed the world. They were not afraid to take risks. They embodied their passions and possessed a knowing that what they were doing was much bigger than whom they are.

What exactly is the role of a CEO? As I pondered this question, I decided to ask Google to see what I could find on the World Wide Web. Thanks to the great innovative resources that have become staples in all of our lives, I came across a good description of what the role of a CEO entails on Wikipedia.

> Typically, the CEO has responsibilities as a director, decision maker, leader, manager and executor. The communicator role can involve the press and the rest of the outside world, as well as the organization's management and employees; the decision-making role involves high-level decisions about policy and strategy. As a leader of the company, the CEO advises the board of directors, motivates employees, and drives change within the organization. As a manager, the CEO presides over the organization's day-to-day operations.

There are CEOs from all walks of life, and they run all different kind of businesses. There are the famous CEOs such as those mentioned above; there are the CEOs who fly low under the radar. But each and every one carries the responsibility of the day-to-day operations to keep the ship he or she is sailing on course.

As a business, our lives have day-to-day operations that need the careful watch of a chief executive officer, one who makes sure all departments have what is needed to create balance and a sense of well-being.

Running Your Life as a Business

Running a business is a complex task, one that requires strong leadership, especially through times of growth and expansion. There are many ways to structure a business. For the sake of this chapter, we will use the example of a company with several departments like operations, management, sales, and human resources. Each department has an effect on the other, so they all need to function harmoniously for a successful outcome. This same logic applies to the concept of running your life as a business. Through the course of this chapter, you will evaluate your various departments to make sure that all are receiving the attention needed in order for your life to function harmoniously.

If a business is overly managed and has a deficiency in sales or operations, that business will likely crumble. The same logic applies to our lives, especially these days when it's easy to be heavily skewed in one area and deficient in another. It's important to look at the departments in our lives and the areas that need attention to make the necessary changes so all departments are functioning at their best. For the purpose of this chapter, we will focus on managing the following departments in our lives: body, mind, spirit, families and friends, career, fun, and goals or aspirations. Let's evaluate each department so you can determine where you are out of balance. Let's get your life running like a Fortune 500 company.

The Body

Our physical health is of prime importance in this business called life. Without it, we become unproductive. It is very important to carefully evaluate this department. If you met me a few years ago, you would have seen a woman on a roller-coaster ride with her health. Stress from my real estate business consumed me, and I had no balance in my personal life. I am still a work in progress, but I have learned the value of giving undivided attention to this department. I've also learned that the imbalances in my other departments were directly a factor in harming my health.

I took control over this department by first acknowledging the day-to-day stress I was putting myself under. I am sure many of you reading this can relate! Stress is an epidemic in our world, and it's up to the individual to mitigate the toll it takes on one's health. I also learned the foods I was eating and lack of exercise and mindful activities, such as meditation, were contributing to adrenal fatigue. This means that your body no longer responds to stress as it should. Instead, it is in constant fight-or-flight mode. I experienced daily headaches, weight gain that I could not get rid of, acne, and constant fatigue. I could sleep ten hours a night and wake up tired. I went to doctor after doctor, who all wanted to treat the symptoms instead of finding the cause.

In my desperate search for relief, I discovered *The Virgin Diet Book* by JJ Virgin. This book discusses all the foods that cause inflammation in the body such as sugar, gluten, dairy, soy, and corn. Always being on the go, I'd been eating high processed and unhealthy foods, the exact foods that were causing inflammation in my body and leaving me exhausted. With this newfound knowledge, I paid attention to what I ate and how I felt, and I soon noticed the direct effect food has on my physical well-being. The daily headaches were a result of eating too much gluten, a substance my body couldn't process.

The scary thing is that nowadays our foods are more processed than ever. We can no longer rely on the food industry to supply us with well-balanced and nutritious food. We have to take responsibility, listen to our bodies, and determine how the food we are eating is affecting our health. On my journey to well-being, I learned to love and respect my body instead of ignoring it.

Our bodies are designed to be active, but many of us spend hours sitting behind a desk all day and eat fast food. It's no wonder we are becoming an obese society. After cleaning up our diets, the next step is to incorporate exercise into our lives. Exercise has medically proven effects on the stress levels in our bodies. I will admit I am working on this area. My schedule is so full that exercise usually is the last to get done. When I do exercise, I feel the difference in my body. I feel energized, I have a sense of accomplishment, and my stress levels drop noticeably. Once again, this is a signal for me that my body likes what I am doing.

If you are running yourself ragged, take time to stop and listen to what your body is telling you. It has inherent wisdom, and it will tell you what it does and doesn't like. Nourish this department because, if this department is undernourished, all the other departments will be affected.

The Mind

The mind is powerful beyond our imagination. Our thoughts are the leading forces in the outcomes we experience. According to the Laboratory of Neuro Imaging at UCLA, our brains process around seventy thousand thoughts a day. It's hard to comprehend, but when you think about it, our minds are constantly racing. The challenge is to become aware of the content of our thoughts, particularly those of our circumstances and ourselves.

When I first began to study the law of attraction and paid attention to my thoughts, I was surprised to find that I didn't think too highly of myself. I have always been a fairly confident person who was comfortable in my skin, but when I drew awareness to my thoughts, I found the mind chatter was rather demeaning toward me.

The basis of the law of attraction is that you attract the content of your thoughts into your world. I evaluated my circumstances, and I found that, based on my way of thinking, I was attracting undesirable results. My thoughts were rather self-centered, and I discovered the negative, self-centered conversations I was having with myself throughout the day were keeping me from discovering the purpose I was desperately searching for. I learned that, in order to truly show up and truly be the best you can be, you must change your internal dialogue. You must love and respect yourself before you can love and respect others.

In *Wishes Fulfilled*, Wayne Dyer discusses the conversation we have with ourselves before we go to bed and how that conversation is what our subconscious marinates in for eight hours. We don't want to be marinating in self-loathing and what we did wrong and don't have. The subconscious doesn't know what is reality and what is just a thought, so our thoughts are processed as if we are living that experience. Hence, we become what we think about. Be mindful of your thoughts, the conversations you have with yourself, and what you think about before you fall to sleep. Marinate in loving and uplifting thoughts.

Meditation is to your mind what exercise is to your body. The article "Meditation Health Benefits: What the Practice Does to Your Body" states the following:

Studies show that meditation is associated with
improvement in a variety of psychological areas,
including stress, anxiety, addiction, depression, eating
disorders and cognitive function, among others. There's
also research to suggest that meditation can reduce
blood pressure, pain response, stress hormone levels
and even cellular health. But what does it actually do to
the body? For one thing, it changes our brain. The cells
and neurons in the brain are constantly making new
connections and disrupting old ones based on response to
stimuli, a quality that researchers call experience-based
neuroplasticity. This affects the neural circuits of the
brain, which in turn affects how we respond to situations.
It also affects the actual structure of our brains—
thickening some areas and making others less dense.

I have incorporated a daily meditation practice, and I have found it to be tremendously helpful in not only setting the tone for the day but also giving me the energy I need to get through my day. I was not aware of the toll stress had been taking on me for years. Meditation has become a big part of the healing process, allowing me to be present and benefit from the healing powers of this practice. I encourage you to try it. I recommend the Omvana app by Mind Valley. You can find it on iTunes, and it has a variety of meditations so you can pick what works best for you.

The Spirit

Our spirit is another department that we need to bring attention to. I found myself on a spiritual journey when I began to study the law of attraction. I wanted to learn how to attract more money in my life and how to attract the material possessions I thought I needed in order to be happy, but what I soon found is that what I thought I needed wasn't the source of happiness. Instead, I aligned myself with spirit, and the universe began to open doors. I experienced happiness within myself.

Living a spirit-filled life is about being aware that our life is a journey, and through our experiences, we learn and grow. I believe we are a spirit having a physical experience. It's hard not to get caught up in the business of day-to-day life, but if we place too much attention there, we begin to separate from spirit. We live in a world that has an underlying basis of fear. My connection with spirit deepened when I developed the understanding that we are all connected. This understanding forms the foundation of my purpose of being of service to others, and it's a purpose that literally everyone can experience. I discovered that, by living from a place of oneness, I began to look at everyone differently and learned to respect their individual journeys, as they too are learning their life lessons in this worldly experience.

The key processes in discovering the essence of spirit are removing judgment, having compassion and forgiveness, and expressing love. To remove judgment, it is important to understand that we are all connected and judgment is fear within ourselves showing up. We must have compassion for everything and everyone. When you are compassionate to the journeys that others are experiencing, you begin to find ways that you can be of service. You can offer your light to those who may need your unique gifts.

Forgiveness is the process of letting go. When you hold a grudge or anger toward someone, the only person it truly affects is the person who is holding on. The process of forgiveness allows you to acknowledge the emotions felt, and in finding peace, you release the energy that has been blocking you from letting go. When you express forgiveness, you offer yourself freedom. The expression of love is a process of increasing your vibration frequency, and it will release any fear that may be present.

In *Power vs. Force*, Dr. David Hawkins illustrates the scale of consciousness ranging from twenty to one thousand. The energy of love vibrates at a frequency of five hundred, whereas the energy of fear vibrates at the energy of one hundred. Fear and love cannot co-exist. When you approach all you do with the basis of love, you close the door to the fears that can become paralyzing.

Friends and Family

Some of us have loving relationships with our families, while others have relationships that trouble us. This department is all about managing how those relationships affect you and the steps that can be taken to not be impacted by those not-so loving relationships or moments. Family dynamics are often complex, and family members can be critical. Sometimes, they want the best for you, and they are naturally protective. And sometimes, there may be instances where you have a family member who doesn't want you to succeed. He or she feels competitive, jealous, or insecure within himself or herself, and he or she can't support your success because he or she is living in fear.

We can't choose our family, but we can manage how our interactions with them impact us. My mom is a nurse and has always been very protective. I have been a risk taker. When I would tell my mom about something I wanted to do, she never responded with excitement or enthusiasm, but caution. I used to get upset by this, but as I learned the importance of not letting the opinion of others, especially your family, affect you, I began to accept that this is one of my mom's characteristics. I now love and appreciate her concerns.

Friends are our adopted family. They are the people who come into our lives by choice. Friends can have tremendous impact on our worlds. Some can be loving and supportive, while others can be competitive and hurtful. I've had experiences with both kinds of friends. I have found there are a rare few that you find that love you unconditionally. Those are the friends you hang on to and cherish. With the friends who are competitive and not supportive, acknowledge the lesson that friendship brought into your life, and then move on. Once again, those people can only affect you as much as you allow them to.

When you experience success and are happy, you might have some jealous friends. Jealously is a low frequency emotion. The key is realizing that, when someone is jealous, he or she is caught up in his or her own interpretation of an event, his or her own story. It has nothing to do with you.

Jealousy is an insecurity that needs to be healed. Even though it is hard not to take it personally when someone who you thought was your friend begins to show that he or she is envious of you, remember that we are each experiencing our individual journey and we have control over the outcome by how we respond to those experiences. It takes practice, but if you can respond to your friend with love and compassion, you won't be as impacted by his or her negative energy.

When evaluating your family and friendships to make sure this department is well balanced, look at the experiences you have, and give gratitude for those relationships that are uplifting and supportive. Forgive those that are not. Be present in the moments that you come together with your loved ones. Enjoy those moments as if they are the last because, in this world, we are only guaranteed the present.

Career

Our careers can be a dominant department in our lives. This is good except when it is to the detriment of the others. Most of us dream about what we will do when we are young and then plan for college and career when we are in our teenage years. Some career plans arise quite naturally. Others are saddled with the expectations of family or upbringing. Once our careers are launched, many of us become consumed with them. Relationships with friends and family are put on the back burner. Now is the time to balance the energies and intentions we bring to this department.

Through experience, I've learned that, when you truly love what you do, balance naturally occurs. I have worked in sales for a long time, and I struggled with the expectations, processes, and competiveness of the industry. I had a hard time finding balance because I was working constantly to not let anyone down. When I travelled, my work went with me. When I was at home after a long day, instead of relaxing and restoring my energy, thoughts of work lingered. It was hard not to get caught up in the competitive nature of sales. I've had many moments in my career where I was just plain burned out. My motivation suffered, my desire to give it all would fluctuate, and at times, I experienced resentment. I struggled to find my passion and purpose.

I experienced a complete shift in my career when I discovered my purpose among the chaos, the production goals, and the need to be number one. When I dedicated my life to being of service, balance found me, and old beliefs that I had been harboring for years began to drift away. When I decided to make my production goals secondary to being of service, I experienced a newfound love for my career, an excitement I didn't have in years and an ease to the way I conducted my business life. I found I could spend half the time on work as I did in the years previous, and my production continued to go up.

Balance is easy to obtain when time no longer is a factor. I let go of the beliefs that I carried about my production, and my stress levels dropped. I found I was able to go on the road with my work, be more productive, and have amazing experiences simultaneously. My perception of those I was working with changed because they no longer were a way to make ends meet, but an opportunity to serve a purpose.

Fun

Fun is frequently one of the most neglected departments in our lives. Having fun is usually what we do to reward ourselves when we have done a good job or when we feel satisfied with our production. But I suggest you plan vacations, nights out with friends, and time for your other interests—movies, rock climbing, painting, mountain biking, whatever they may be—regardless of your satisfaction level at work. I used to feel guilty about indulging in vacations or nights out if I weren't meeting the benchmarks I'd set for myself or if my sales weren't up to par.

When I did go on a vacation, I inevitably took along my work and couldn't enjoy myself until I had spent a little time on something related to my business. This is why I loved vacations in Hawaii. I couldn't relax until the workday ended back home, and when offices in Utah were closing, I still had several hours of daylight to enjoy on the beach in Hawaii.

Since my career has come into balance and I found purpose through being of service, I have become more laid back. I'm able to turn off my mind and really be in the present moment when I need a recharge.

I recently took up mountain biking. My good friend had been mountain biking for about a year, and she kept prompting me to try it. In my search for fun activities that would allow my mind to take a break, I decided to give it a shot. The only bad thing I have to say about it is, "Why didn't I start sooner?" It allows me to be outside, get a physical workout, and concentrate on the task at hand. You have to focus just on your ride, or you begin to drift off track, which will cause you to wreck. It's fun and relaxing, and it's a great de-stressor!

Find that thing that allows you to mentally focus on the moment and task at hand. Having a mental vacation regularly is hard to do, but when you can find that activity that allows you to have fun and clear your mind, you'll become addicted in a good way. It's your escape and way to welcome more balance into your life.

When you have fun and let loose from time to time, you will find that the energy you project is light and filled with joy instead of overworked and stuffy. Now, who would you rather be around, someone fun and light or overworked and stuffy?

Goals and Aspirations

We all have goals or things we aspire to or wish to accomplish. They are often the driving forces in our lives, and we usually begin the year with a list of New Year's resolutions to bring about the changes we desire. Have you ever gone back and compared your resolutions to the year before? How many did you actually accomplish, and how many are reoccurring resolutions? Most of my resolutions haunted me year after year, and making the list was just a reminder of the things I didn't accomplish the year before. It was getting depressing.

Instead of these ironclad resolutions, I now put together a list of fun and uplifting things I'd like to try each year. I also allow the list to change throughout the year, as I am somewhat spontaneous and find it exciting to do something unexpected. When it comes time to reflect on the list, it's not about what I didn't do, but rather what brought me joy.

As business owners and salespeople, we also have goals, and we map out the year and our expectations. I used to live by the business outline for my production levels. I would compare it every month, and time after time, I felt disappointed in myself because I didn't meet the standards I had set for myself, criteria that were often extreme.

I changed the format of my business plan when I discovered my purpose. Now I don't base my annual goals on how much I am going to make or how many transactions I am going to close, but simply on how many people I can help. When I made this change, my production naturally increased, and it was a testament to how powerful the law of attraction really is. I learned that, when I worked from a place of gratitude for my opportunity, purpose, and clients, I magnetically attracted more opportunities that increased my production and numbers. I have since been able to decrease time spent on my work, release stress from my world, and find peace and happiness in being of service to others.

We underestimate the power of our intentions. When they are aligned with service and we are in a place of giving, we open ourselves to be in a place of receiving. When we outline our year, either through resolutions or business plans, we attach ourselves to the outcomes. And when our plans don't work out as we outlined, we are disappointed. When you work from a place of being in service and there is no outcome to attach to that is when the universe responds.

We've covered all the departments in our business called life. Where do you need more, and where are you too heavily askew? What changes will you make to create a balance in all departments of your life so your life will run like a Fortune 500 company?

Take a moment now to digest the ideas presented in this chapter and think about what we have uncovered. Then apply the 4 × 4 Method to become the CEO of your life.

1. Identify becoming the CEO of your life. Ask yourself challenge questions:
   1. What does being the CEO of your life mean to you?
   2. What situations make you feel you are being the CEO of your life?
   3. What situations make you feel you are not the CEO of your life?
   4. How would you rate your ability to be the CEO of your life on a scale from one to ten?

2. Identify the types of obstacles that are in your path to be the CEO of your life. Please write four examples. This will help identify what needs to be cleared. For example, "I resent not having a balance in my life."
   1.

    2.

    3.

    4.

3. Follow the steps to help clear obstacles for the ultimate CEO of your life! Here you are bringing about the change:

    1. Identify your earliest memory that formed your beliefs about having balance in your life. For example, "You can't have it all".

    2. If your beliefs are positive and balance-based, praise your experience, and honor them. Write it out. If you find your early experiences toward balance are negative and ego-based, write how you would have preferred it to be.

    3. Visualize yourself as the CEO of your life, embracing that younger you and wonderful experience of having balance and a fulfilled life.

    4. Give thanks for the new awareness. Post a note where you will be able to see it to remind you regularly that you are living a balanced, abundant, and fulfilled life!

4. State your goal/intention for creating the frequency of leading a balanced and fulfilled life. Write the opposite to your list of obstacles here. Now it is time to create! For example, "I am grateful for the balance in my life and that it is possible to have it all."

    1.

    2.

    3.

    4.

CHAPTER 4

Confidence

Go confidently in the direction of your
dreams. Live the life you've imagined.

—Henry David Thoreau

As it begins to become clear that the process of experiencing transformation is an inward journey, we must do the work on the inside in order to see changes in our outside world. Let's start to dig even deeper to begin the transformation from a sales agent to a service agent in discussing confidence.

For the last ten years of my sales career, I have been searching for meaning outside of my work. I longed for a deeper sense of purpose. Though I was making a good living, I knew there had to be more than leads, prospects, and building up the pipeline. Through trial and error, I learned that having confidence in my abilities, product, and service was secondary to what I discovered to be the core of my mission.

Let's dive into this mission by examining the career path you have chosen and ways that confidence plays a role in the outcomes you are experiencing. Having confidence as a salesperson separates the good salespeople from the great. You must understand your product inside and out. You must be the conduit between you and what your client seeks. What's interesting about confidence, however, is others' perceptions of it.

Throughout this chapter, we will be discussing the following topics, ways they relate to confidence, and some tools and techniques that will offer you support in your transformation:

- External Confidence
- Internal Confidence
- Clearing Stuck Energy
- Applying the Law of Attraction
- Having a New Awareness
- Simply Service

External Confidence

A person with external confidence is most often recognized as being arrogant, egotistical, or boastful. I am sure you have met individuals like this, especially in the highly competitive sales industry, which is often referred to as being cutthroat. It's hard to not feel the urge to be arrogant, egotistical, or boastful when you are swimming with the sharks. Is it possible that insecurities are hiding behind these mannerisms? The answer to this question is, in my opinion, yes. This is likely to happen when a salesperson draws his or her self-assurance from external things such as driving the most expensive car, wearing the latest and greatest fashion, or having the best sales record for the year. Does this type of confidence actually carry with it a true security, or is it merely a security blanket?

How do you think a customer perceives external confidence? No one wants to feel like he or she is responsible for your next Mercedes or trip to Hawaii. External confidence is what I like to refer to as a crutch. It is a form of confidence that is outside of us and outside of our control. It can become the creation of a codependent relationship.

Internal Confidence

Have you ever met a person who drew you in the instant he or she made eye contact with you or said hello? Have you ever met someone who immediately made you feel at ease? When he or she spoke to you, he or she was present, engaged, and genuinely ready to move a mountain to help you. A person with this form of confidence is the exact opposite of someone who is boastful or arrogant.

My definition of internal confidence means you possess the ability to be comfortable in any situation and have ease in whatever you do. You embody an unconditional love for yourself. Love is the basis for everything you do. You have the ability to separate yourself from the opinion of others and possess an acceptance that they are only opinions. You always make those you encounter feel uplifted by your presence.

A person with internal confidence knows whom he or she is and isn't motivated by external circumstances. When you know your purpose and are aligned with it, there is ease to connecting with your client that no sales training course can ever teach you.

Material abundance has been important to me over the years, but I don't think I ever felt the sense of peace, joy, and love that has come to me since I embraced being in service as a key component in my sales work. I'm not saying that someone who gains confidence from external sources is untrustworthy or a bad person; however, what I hope to have you explore is the difference between these two types of confidence. Then you discern which source of confidence feels better to you. Which form of confidence do you think would foster a richer relationship with your client? How would you like to be the one that lights up the room when you walk in just by being you? How do you think your customers will respond when they feel the light and love exuding from you as you work with them?

Take a few minutes to reflect on the distinction between these two types of confidence and see if your confidence comes from within or from external sources. As I said earlier, it is not a bad thing to find confidence in your external world, but bringing this fact to your awareness gives you an opportunity to recognize the source of your confidence and look within for validation. The shift in energy can truly be life changing.

I want to share a personal story that made me aware that I was drawing my confidence from an external source. When I finally realized this, I was able to shift to an internal source for my confidence. The impact on my life has been profound.

When I was an impressionable twelve years old, I ran around with a group of friends whom I found somewhat intimidating. They were very outspoken about material possessions. I found myself envious of what they had. As much as I could, I tried to keep up. When the school year started, my new friends had all the bells and whistles. They talked about their name brand jeans and how they had so many new outfits that they didn't need to wear anything twice for a month. I didn't say much during these conversations. I wasn't embarrassed. Once again, I was envious.

One day in music class, one of my friends asked me, "Didn't you already wear those jeans this week?"

I was a little stunned and mortified because I didn't want them to know that I did already wear them. They were LA Jeans, my favorites. I replied, "No, I have two pairs of these jeans."

She laughed and said, "I don't know anyone who would buy two of the same pair of jeans, and I don't believe you. I think you wore them this week already."

I don't recall how the rest of the conversation went, but after that day, I never wore the same jeans or outfit twice in the same week. I was devastated and embarrassed by the fact that my wardrobe was used to judge me as inferior.

If we fast-forward to my twenties, my wardrobe choices now mattered a great deal to me. My confidence was directly related to my outfit. I spent a lot of time and money building my very own independent-woman's wardrobe and found myself almost twenty thousand dollars in debt due to this form of expression.

It was not until recently that I became aware that this belief, where I associated my confidence with dressing to impress, had been carried forward from that incident as a young teenager to the present day. I still enjoy the finer things in fashion, and I will appreciate any great outfit, but it is no longer my source of confidence. I am much more responsible with my spending habits. Prior to my new awareness, I still felt the emotions I had that day. Now, after having had the realization, I am in a neutral place with the memory, and I am thankful for the lesson.

I know this is a silly example, but when you are getting reacquainted with yourself, you will find that instances that seemed minor actually had a substantial impact on your life and you carried forward beliefs that created undesirable outcomes. It's empowering to come face-to-face with those moments, be able to rewrite your story, and bid farewell to the old beliefs that no longer serve a purpose for you.

Clearing Stuck Energy

When you come face-to-face with those moments, as I did with my example of attributing my confidence with how I dressed, we can experience certain emotions or discover that those old stories continue to repeat themselves. We find ourselves in cycles that we don't know how to break.

A good example is when you hear someone talk about that he or she continues to attract the wrong partners who all seem to be alike. This is a product of having a story that continues to replay itself. We have to bring that story to the forefront in order to fully understand why and where this story originated. We all have had unpleasant experiences we know that were unpleasant because we relive the emotions we felt during that experience as we recall them through our memories.

Take a moment, and think back on your life and a time that was challenging, painful, or fearful. It doesn't have to be a catastrophic event. It can be something that happened when you were a child or during an impressionable time in your life. Regardless of how big or small, the point is that it's still hanging around. It has a conscious or unconscious effect on your life. Close your eyes, and take note of what comes to mind first. How do you feel when you reflect on the incident? What emotion were you feeling? Does the emotion come back when you recall it? This is a key to help you begin to peel the layers of how and where you find your confidence. You may want to repeat this process multiple times as you begin the journey of having this new awareness.

What we have to do as these things come back to our awareness is to decipher the lesson to be learned and move through the emotion until we are in a neutral place with it. The key is to access the emotion during times of reflection. It can be hard because most negative emotions are suppressed. This process is called clearing.

Emotions are energy in motion, and in some cases, if we don't fully process the emotions, they can get stuck. They will hang out until a particular event triggers that emotion and brings it to the surface again to process. How do you know when an issue has been cleared? It occurs when you are able to come to a neutral place over that thing that was very hurtful or made you angry at one time. It is an emotional but very liberating process. As you continue to do the reflection exercise, you will find that random things may come to mind, along with events you have not thought about in years. Allow those thoughts to surface. Go back and feel that experience again. You may even get emotional or angry all over again. Allow yourself to process these emotions and let the clearing begin.

If you want help with the process of energy clearing, I recommend visiting www.hiwattliving.com. You will find more information on energy clearing and have access to someone who can help you clear the energy that is no longer serving you.

Applying the Law of Attraction

Now that we have identified the two categories of confidence and have a method on how to clear stuck energy, let's talk about the law of attraction and ways we can apply it. A simple explanation of the law of attraction is "like attracts like." Focus on positive thoughts, and welcome those into your life. Dwell on all that is not working in your life. Yes, more of that is sure to arrive or continue to linger. There are many ways to apply the law of attraction into our daily lives.

In this case, we are evaluating how the law of attraction is applicable when we are identifying the source of our confidence, whether we are deriving it from an external or internal source. This is important because what we focus on, what motivates us, and what our intentions are may be all a product of our thoughts and, in turn, what we are attracting into our world. This may be a new concept to some, but it's empowering to have this knowledge. Knowing we can truly change the circumstances of our lives by solely adjusting the content of our thoughts is a great source of freedom.

Look at your business or career. What do you do and don't like about it? In a perfect world, what would it look like? How would it be different from what it is now? When you started on this path, what were your intentions with it? Was it to make more money? Was it because your dream was to be in this line of work? Or was it the best thing you could find?

So many of us just settled because we decided to undervalue ourselves. How many of you can say you chose this direction because it was an avenue to be of service or one to improve lives—yours, your family's, and the people you encounter every day? What are your intentions behind your motivation? Are they self-serving, or do you have the intention to apply your knowledge, talents, abilities, and products to be of service to your clients? Which do you think would feel better?

I wanted to bring this to your awareness because it is an important part in understanding the power behind what we are thinking about. In turn, it has a direct effect on the actions we take when creating our reality.

Having a New Awareness

Let's take a moment to apply this newfound knowledge and compare the ideas of coming from a place of external or internal confidence. What sort of limitations are you placing on yourself if you gain confidence externally? What sort of doubts or worries creep into your mind if you gain confidence from something outside of yourself? Maybe you feel comfortable and confident when you are with your group of friends. What if your friends moved away or started new relationships that took their time away from you? What effect would that have on you and your confidence? If your friends were removed from the equation, would you be able to act or behave the same as if your friends were there?

We live in a world that puts a lot of emphasis on what others think or say about us. With the rise of social media, positive or negative opinions can be expressed to the world. Many of us allow those opinions to creep into our minds and create insecurities, which then create the cycle of finding external sources of comfort, reassurance, or temporary happiness. When applying the principle that you become what you focus on, is it possible that, if you are always in a state of fear, doubt, or worry, you could create undesirable circumstances? Yes! In the event that our confidence is acquired outside of ourselves, where does that leave us when our security blanket is no longer present? What sorts of circumstances do you think you would begin to create in your sales business or career? And what would your client base look like?

When we derive our confidence from within—when we are secure within ourselves and the decisions we have made and we feel at peace—fear, doubt, and worry can't take hold. Here we understand that our lives are a reflection of our thoughts. Once this awareness is in the forefront, we are careful about what we allow into our mind-set. The beauty of being in this space is that, no matter what situation you are in, what deadlines you have, or who is sitting across from you, you are confident in your abilities, message, and intentions. You don't have to be labeled the top producer or drive a fancy car to feel empowered.

Simply Service

So how we can make the necessary shifts in our thoughts and actions to be in a place where faith in oneself arises from within?

Every life experience, whether large or small, shapes us today. We have to know and acknowledge that we are not victims in life, but we are here to learn a purpose, and our life path takes us in so many different directions. Each direction is to teach us a lesson, which aligns us with our higher self or purpose. Our confidence is the energy that emanates from us. We as humans have a sense that enables us to pick up and feel the energy of those we are around.

Keep this in mind because it all begins with our thoughts. If we gain our confidence from a crutch, something outside of us, what happens to our confidence when our crutch is not present? What happens if we are in a moment that is "make or break" for our business or career? Do you want to be internally confident, or do you want to be sweating bullets because you left your confidence in the parking lot? Looking within and building your confidence based on love for yourself, what you do, and your purpose; a knowledge of who you are; and an awareness that you are on purpose could be your "make or break" moment. This is not an easy task to accomplish, and we will spend our lives changing courses, which at times could shake our confidence, but having the light within that will never go out will be life changing.

When you have the awareness of what you are putting out energetically, you can begin to apply this in your business practice. When you introduce an intention of service and become truly in service to your client, don't you think he or she will energetically notice that energy? You will create a magnetic draw to yourself of others who are seeking what you are putting out energetically.

Now look at it from the standpoint that everyone you encounter is viewed as another deal, a chance to make more money. How do you think that will feel energetically? I have personally experienced this shift back and forth in my business. I know for a fact that you tend to be much more magnetic when you are in a genuine place of service. These very experiences compelled me to share these business-changing approaches.

As we begin to shift our awareness and apply service as a top priority into the sales process, how does this concept tie to confidence? Let me share with you another personal example to put it in perspective.

Of my twenty years of sales experience, the last ten have been in real estate sales. I have had the pleasure of attending many training seminars and classes promoting the latest, greatest, quickest, and best way to build your business. Most of these classes focused on how much money could be made by applying specific tools such as cold calling and door knocking. These basic techniques translate into the concept of approaching as many people as you can and in as many ways that you can to see if they are ready to buy or sell real estate.

Sales is a numbers game, and those who have followed these tools and techniques have many success stories. Still, I felt uneasy following these techniques. I thought about how I would feel getting these phone calls or being approached in these various matters. I did not like it, so I struggled through the live classes and live call sessions.

One class really stood out to me. We were in a bullpen setting, an open area with cubicles set up with phone stations. On that day, we were making cold calls to generate real estate leads. I struggled throughout most of the day because I was just plain uncomfortable. The coach who was working the room seemed to make quite a few stops at my station. He would plug into my calls, which caused me to immediately freeze up.

After a couple times, he pulled me aside and said, "You sound scared to death, you sound like a robot on the phone, and it's no wonder you are not getting any appointments. You need to stand up straight and put a smile on your face."

I must have had a deer in the headlights look on my face because he said, "Get your script book, and you will go over and over the script until you sound like you are being personable and not an automated machine."

Once he was satisfied with my tone, he said something that resonated with me and has become the driving force in my business since that very moment. "Don't put so much pressure on yourself. You are here to help people. You happen to help those in need of real estate services. Not everyone may need your service at this time, but that's okay. You are just looking for the next person you may be of service to."

A wave of relief came over me! He was right. I was here to be of service. It finally clicked that my purpose was solely to assist those who needed my help and making these phone calls was a simple way to let the person on the other end know I was there to help. His advice completely turned around my day, and I ended up making fifteen appointments. It opened the door to my discovery of what was missing in my business. The purpose I was so desperately seeking outside of my business and my daily activities was actually right under my nose.

As we wrap up the conversation on confidence, I want you to really think. Does your confidence come from something tangible or intangible? If you were put on the spot, how would your confidence hold up? Or would you be crying inside for your blanket? When your business or career is based on sales, you will find that there are many "make or break" moments when you are put on the spot regularly.

Identify what makes you feel like you could take over the world, and if doesn't come from within, it's time to do some soul searching. It's time to look within yourself and see what you have been missing all this time.

As you begin to release the ideas, beliefs, or experiences that no longer serve you, opportunities will appear for you to be of service to everyone you encounter. As you make the shifts in your intentions, you will find fulfillment in your daily routine. This is exceptionally empowering, and it allows us individually as salespersons to have an impact by doing what we do best. One at a time, we can change our industry and community. And hey, why stop there? Let's change the world!

Take a moment now to digest and think about what we have uncovered and then apply the 4 × 4 Method to cultivate our internal confidence.

1. Identify internal confidence. Ask yourself challenge questions:
   1. What does internal confidence mean to you?
   2. What situations make you feel confident?
   3. In which situations do you feel a lack of confidence?
   4. How would you rate your internal confidence on a scale from one to ten?

2. Identify the types of obstacles that are in your path to achieve inner confidence. List four examples. This will help identify what needs to be cleared. For example, "Speaking in front of a group is frightening."
   1.
   2.
   3.
   4.

3. Follow these steps to help clear obstacles for your ultimate confident you! Here you are bringing about the change.
   1. Identify your earliest memory that formed your belief about your internal confidence (positive or negative).
   2. If it's positive, praise your experience and honor it. Write it out. If it's negative, write how you would have preferred it to go.
   3. Visualize yourself within the positive scenario, embracing that younger you and new wonderful experience of glorious internal confidence.
   4. Give thanks for the new awareness. Post a note where you will be able to see it to remind you regularly that abundant and fulfilling internal confidence fills you!

4. State your goal/intention for creating the frequency of inner confidence. Write the opposite of your list of obstacles. Now it is time to create! For example, "I am an articulate and confident public speaker!"

   1.
   2.
   3.
   4.

CHAPTER 5

Rejection

A rejection is nothing more than a necessary
step in the pursuit of success.

—Bo Bennett

Rejection is an everyday occurrence in the trenches of the sales world. Rejection typically is not pleasant and can be taken personally. It's not surprising that we take steps to avoid rejection, as it literally keeps many of us from picking up the phone to make that call, submitting our ideas, or approaching that big customer.

How does rejection have the ability to make us feel so uneasy at times? A study by Naomi Eisenberger, PhD, at the University of California, Los Angeles; Kipling Williams, PhD, at Purdue University; and colleagues found that social rejection activates many of the same brain regions involved in physical pain (*Science* 2003). No wonder we are as apt to avoid rejection, as we are to avoid circumstances that may lead to physical pain. Taking into consideration that rejection not only is an everyday part of the sales world but also is likely to occur in all aspects of life, let's tackle the topic of rejection by exploring the following ideas:

- They Are Only Opinions
- Don't Take It Personally
- Break Free of the Fear of Rejection

They Are Only Opinions

What is it about our society that has us put so much emphasis on the opinion and approval of others? And how does this apply to being rejected? With advances in technology and the ability to communicate 24-7, everyone has an opinion and numerous opportunities to express it. Many times, these statements can come across as confrontational or lacking consideration of the recipient. It is human nature to desire the acceptance of those in our social circles and business atmospheres, so we post, tweet, and Google, constantly checking to see how we are perceived online. This internal need for acceptance can be paralyzing.

It's easy to be influenced by the opinion of others, but the key is to remember that it is just an opinion. An opinion is solely a perception of another person. Everyone's perception is different. Let's reframe rejection as an opinion that contradicts one of our own. It shouldn't be taken personally, and it shouldn't interfere with forward progress. Understand that, when confronted with an opposing opinion, it is only an opinion.

Don't Take It Personally

Why do we take rejection personally? This is related to the need to feel accepted, that is, the need to have a place within our social circle or business. Someone saying no to us typically isn't a form of personal rejection, though it's often internalized that way. In sales, "no" is a word we hear often. Our ability to hear that dreaded response and to be able to continue on is a key factor in the rise or fall of one's sale career.

We have to able to remove ourselves from the place of fear where we are usually trapped when confronted with rejection. This is a liberating process and is accomplished by adopting a newfound internal confidence and shifting the intention behind what we are setting out to accomplish in our day job. This allows you to be comfortable when you are told no, that is, when someone does not need your product or service at a particular time. It's all in your presentation, speech, package, or product, whatever it maybe.

When you are 100 percent in a place of service, you will be in a place of peace when your business proposal or sales pitch is rejected. This is nothing personal, and it should never keep you from making that phone call, doing that presentation, or offering your services.

Break Free of the Fear of Rejection

There are many examples in history of those who were able to overcome rejection. They continued with an intention, passion, and understanding that it was simply a part of the process. Thomas Edison's famous quote says, "I have not failed. I have just found ten thousand ways that don't work."

What if he had stopped after the first or second attempt? His contribution to the world was tremendous, and his ability to persevere should be an inspiration to everyone. How many wonderful ideas or contributions to the world have never taken flight because the mastermind behind them experienced rejection or had a fear of being a failure? Would you rather take a risk and persevere or live your life wondering what would have happened if you had tried?

We are only great if we allow ourselves to be. Greatness is not born because of the opinion of others. Greatness is born when we decide to take a chance, make a change, and have a tireless belief and passion around our purpose.

This is relative to the business and sales world because there are literally millions of people from different cultures and backgrounds, all with unique perspectives who have the ability to have a direct effect on many lives. Most of us don't realize the opportunity we have created for ourselves to be of a higher purpose. We just look at our everyday work activities as a way to make ends meet. I am here to tell you now that there is much more to it than that.

How many times have you attempted to try something new or different? In making the attempt, you didn't initially receive the response you had hoped for and decided to scratch the idea and go back to your comfort zone. How many times did you have an idea but talked yourself out it because you were worried about how it would be received or what others would think about it? We have all been in this position at one time or another. I can think of many times in my life and career when the overbearing mind chatter took over. The anxiety of how I would feel if the worst-case scenario happened kept me from making that phone call. It contributed to my procrastination and inevitably allowed myself to stay where it felt safe. There are countless stories of those who were faced with rejection, and it stopped them dead in their tracks. What end of the spectrum do you want to find yourself?

Allow yourself to feel the anticipation, anxiety, or whatever sensation you experience when confronted with rejection. Make the conscious decision that you have nothing to lose and take a leap of faith. No matter what you are setting out to accomplish, if backed by intentions aligned with something outside of yourself, a higher power, you will reap the rewards by taking that next step. In those moments when you have knots in your stomach, remember what your intentions are. If they are coming from a place of love and service, then rest assured. Everything will be taken care of. It's a powerful tool in helping you take the next step: make that phone call, start that business, or make that career change.

No matter what you are doing with your life, if you find yourself on a path where you are doing something that you enjoy and love and will make you happy, then continue on. You will hit speed bumps, you will come across roadblocks, and you will have doors closed in your face. But don't allow your ego to convince you that it is time to give up. Listen to what is within you and what is driving the love for what you do. We have an opportunity to make a difference in the world. It can be one woman, man, child, or animal at a time, or it can be the masses. Whatever it may be, we all have a purpose, making the world a better place.

Start by taking a good look at the business or career path you have chosen. In what way is following that career path or working in that business contributing to making the world a better place? What is the service message? The universe responds to our needs when we place ourselves in a position to carry out the act of love. This act can be done in many ways.

We have an opportunity to take ourselves out of the equation and do what is in the best and highest interest of those we are of service to. And in doing so, we can be assured that our needs will be met. This occurs as long as we are aligned with the frequency of our highest intentions. When you are in place of leading from the highest good, fear and rejection no longer can exist in your world.

There will be a point in time when we will reflect on how we have evolved. The memories of fear and rejection are gentle reminders as to the power of our thoughts and actions. This will occur when we have made the shift to internal confidence and change in our intentions to be of service. We have to be compassionate as we reflect on our past choices and actions. We have all felt out of place and uncomfortable. We've all thought we blew it at times. We've had many experiences when people have said no to us. The beauty of those experiences is that we learned from them.

When we look at it from this perspective, it can be a relief to know that, without those uncomfortable moments, we wouldn't be who we are today. If life were without challenges and heartache, what would the world be like? When you think of this world as a place that gives us an opportunity to grow and persevere, it can be quite motivating and inspiring to just roll with the punches. This opens a window of opportunity to look back on your life, come face-to-face with your failed attempts, and ask, "What lesson did I learn?"

Trust what comes to mind when you ask yourself that question. This can be quite profound. Not only will it contribute to you being in a place of having peace of mind or closure, it will also clear the energy and allow the blocks to your life purpose to be removed.

I would like to share a personal story about my fear of rejection and the way it played a role in my sales career. In my early twenties, I was living in Las Vegas. I had received a promotion at work, and I was asked to be on the sales team to market and sell a real estate investment fund. The company I was working for was evolving, and the owner saw an opportunity to raise money from private investors to fund construction projects throughout Las Vegas. The company decided to structure it as a securities offering, and I was able to participate in the process that an offering of this sort goes through in order to be classified as a registered offering. My previous sales job was in hotel sales so this was quite a drastic change. I felt like I had made it to the big leagues.

I worked very hard to have an understanding of the offering, processes of the registration, fund, projects, and expectations on us once the offering became live. Each of us was assigned certain areas that we would prospect. We would take calls from the advertisers and travel to do live workshops. As the live date got closer, we began to prep our areas. We scheduled the advertising, mail campaigns, and workshops. We didn't have any formal sales training around this project, but it seemed to come naturally.

The day had come, the fund was live, and we all sat in our cubicles, waiting for the phones to start ringing. The morning came and went, and finally after lunch, the phone rang. I picked it up, ready to make a sale.

The voice on the other end of the line said, "I saw the ad in the journal. What can you tell me about this real estate investment you are offering?"

Here we go, I thought.

At that point, everyone was standing around me, anxious to hear how the first sale was going to go. I started to give him the information he requested, and my mind froze. The key words I had become so familiar with escaped me. I stumbled and bumbled. My team was all starting to say stuff to me at once to help me out, and the gentleman on the phone just politely listened.

After I painfully spat out my sales pitch, he asked, "Why don't you go ahead and mail me some information?" Was he still curious, or was this his nice way of saying, "Since you don't seem to know what you are talking about, go ahead and mail me the information?"

I took down his details and hung up the phone. At that point, everyone had returned to his or her corner, and I felt deflated.

The week seemed to drag on. We didn't quite get the response we had all been prepped for, so now what? The following week, we had a sales meeting, and my boss decided it was time to throw some in-office motivation into the equation. Whoever sold the highest percentage of this hundred million-dollar deal was going to get a new car!

After the meeting, my sales manager pulled me aside and said, "It's going to be difficult for you to make sales over the phone because you sound like a little girl."

I just stood there for a minute, wondering what she could be possibly trying to accomplish by giving me this piece of advice. I didn't know what she was doing other than sabotaging my confidence. I knew I was going to have to overcome my age in some instances. I was in my early twenties, and my sales career was just starting. Reflecting on my experience with that first sales call and this advice from someone who I was supposed to look up to, I became extremely nervous on the phone. The fear of rejection took over.

After that experience, I could have easily ended my sales career and ventured out to find something that felt safe, but no, I wasn't going to go down that way. It became my mission to prove my manager wrong, and I am proud to say that I didn't let rejection get the best of me and I found small success in the early stages of my career. I attribute the drive I have today to that experience and lesson on rejection.

From time to time, a fear of rejection still confronts me, and I worry about how my potential clients and colleagues perceive me, but as I shift my viewpoint and focus on my ability to be of service versus making a sale, those insecurities melt away. At times when I feel nervous or intimidated, I remind myself that I have been granted an opportunity to contribute to my community through my business. This is the key to overcoming the fear of rejection. Rejection will not go away, but we can rise above it so it's no longer a defining aspect of our world.

What you put out is what you get back. If you put out service, love, compassion, and joy, then you will get service, love, compassion, and joy in return. Use the setbacks you have experienced to be an inspiration and guide to those you may serve. How refreshing to know that you didn't go through all that crap for nothing!

Take a moment and reflect on your journey and those times when you thought your world was upside down or you had an encounter with a person who seemed to bring out the worst in you. Find the lesson in that experience, and bring it to your awareness. This will give you closure on a higher level.

Let's apply the 4 × 4 Method to bring forth your newfound interpretation on rejection and the peace that comes with this new understanding.

1. How has rejection had an impact on you? Ask yourself the challenge questions:
    1. What does being rejected mean to you?
    2. When have you experienced rejection?
    3. What situations do you avoid because of the fear of rejection?
    4. What dreams have you not taken any action on because of the fear of rejection?

2. Which of your experiences have created a fear that is blocking you from overcoming rejection? Please write four. For example, "My business proposal was rejected."
    1.
    2.
    3.
    4.

3. Follow these steps to help clear blocks to the fearless and compassionate you.
    1. Identify your experiences with rejection that has created this fear.
    2. Identify the lesson you learned or are to learn from that experience. (Remember, go with what comes to mind first. This is typically the answer. It is helpful to close your eyes and ask yourself the question.)
    3. Visualize yourself back in an experience where rejection could potentially be the outcome, and be in a place of peace with no attachment to the outcome.
    4. Give thanks for the new awareness. Post a note where you will be able to see it to remind you regularly that you are fearless, love, and compassionate.

4. State your goal/intention for creating the frequency of peace. Write the opposite to your list of obstacles here. For example, "My business proposal was accepted and received rave reviews.
    1.
    2.
    3.
    4.

CHAPTER 6

Falling in Love with Me

Love is the great miracle cure. Loving
ourselves works miracles in our lives.

—Louis L. Hay

Why do we have such a hard time loving ourselves just the way we are? Self-love is the catalyst in how we show up in our everyday lives, yet most of us barely have any self-love. In this chapter, we talk about the importance of self-love and the reasons why we should lead all we do with self-love. In doing so, we will discover the ways the practice of self-love transforms our business life and all our social interactions. We will discuss the process of falling in love with ourselves, ways to quiet the constant mind chatter that does not serve us, the awareness of thoughts creating reality, and the value of finding love for ourselves sooner than later in the following conversations:

- How You Begin to Fall in Love with Yourself
- Mind Chatter
- Your Reality Is a Mirrored Reflection of Your Thoughts
- Determining Your Value
- Giving and Receiving

How You Begin to Fall in Love with Yourself

A healthy love of self is the first and most important step in committing to lead with the intention of service. It is also, in my opinion, the most avoided and uncomfortable process for most of us. We are not taught as children to love ourselves. We have been conditioned that self-love is a form of bragging and it can come across as egotistical. This lack of self-love has led many of us down a path of limited beliefs—I can't do that, if only, just my luck, why me—costing us our time, efforts, and talents. Most of us don't believe we hold the key to a fulfilling, happy, successful, and abundant life. Think back on a time when you truly patted yourself on the back without a "but" mixed into the congratulations that you offered yourself.

How many times have you had an encounter with someone and the only reflection of that encounter is how you messed it up or made a fool of yourself? How many times do you focus on your failures versus your successes? It's quite scary to think that we are so quick to judge ourselves and allow the opinions of others to determine our destiny.

As a salesperson, there are many opportunities to become our own worst critic, to allow our peers and competitors to get the best of us, and to undervalue our worth. I have experienced it firsthand. In the early years of my sales career, I worked in an environment where I knew that those I worked alongside would rather see me fail than succeed. My success was looked upon as a threat. It's hard to remain optimistic when you are constantly looking over your shoulder. What I know now—and this would have been extremely valuable to me then—is that having an unconditional love for myself allows me not to be rattled in environments like that.

I have always focused on the good in others, even when they are staring me in the face with the hopes that I fall. I used to look at this desire to see good in others as a bad habit I needed to break because I tend to go all in. And oftentimes, I end up with the short end of the stick. I have now learned that seeing the good in others is only to my advantage. Having a perspective of love, compassion, and forgiveness is truly the key to thriving in any circumstance.

The journey I have been on in seeking, discovering, and developing my self-love has been filled with many ups and downs. It's not a simple process, but it's one of the most important things that you will ever do. It's a process of pushing through your limited beliefs, being okay with looking at yourself in the mirror, and saying with ease, "I love you."

So how do you begin to fall in love with yourself? There is no right or wrong way to do so. It's a matter of what feels right for you. The key is being genuine about it. It feels silly at first and a little uncomfortable, and your family or friends may wonder why you are standing in front of a mirror telling yourself, "I love you."

We all have something we would like to change about ourselves. Most of us don't like the sound of our own voices, and there is a reason why the diet industry is a billion-dollar industry. We are all looking for that magic pill, quick fix, or get-rich-quick plan in order to experience happiness. What we don't realize is that we need to find happiness in the present. Happiness is not a product of what we have or how we look, yet this is how most of us define our happiness. The concept of finding happiness in the present is key when wanting to experience life-changing shifts.

I am a planner by nature. I map out everything in every moment in my life. The idea of being in the present took a lot of practice for me, and I am still a work in progress. I have perpetually planned my next steps and always been mindful of where I was going and not where I was in the moment. This is a tricky balance because we all have to be mindful of our path and also be present. As an experienced salesperson, I was always two to three months ahead of myself and sometimes six months to a year. How many of you can relate? Time seemed to always escape me. I could be having a conversation with someone and literally not hear a word he or she said because my mind was in planning mode, calculating my next moves.

I am still very much a planner, but I've become aware of the benefits of taking a moment and stepping back. When I discovered my purpose through being of service, I found this an extremely important step in allowing myself to be in a flow. Because I was so much a planner when something did not work out as I had planned, I would place blame on myself or belittle myself, even though things were out of my control most of the time. I was not easy on myself. Now, how many of you can relate? We tend to be our own worst critics. In that moment of stepping back, I learned how to be gentle with myself.

Falling in love with you starts with being present. What does it mean to fully be present? In *The Power of Now*, Eckhart Tolle writes,

> Time isn't precious at all, because it is an illusion. What
> you perceive as precious is not time but the one point
> that is out of time: the Now. That is precious indeed. The
> more you are focused on time-past and future-the more
> you miss the Now, the most precious thing there is.

This is profound because we can't change the past. The past is the past, and we have no control over the future because it could change at the drop of a hat. How many times have you gone into the office with your day mapped out, only to have a client pop in? Or you receive a call that takes you off task, or a family emergency comes up unexpectedly. My stress levels used to rise rapidly if things didn't go as planned. Daily stress took a toll on my body, and I ended up developing stress-related illnesses.

It wasn't until I was able to understand the concept of being in the moment, being present, and allowing the unexpected to just be that I was able to reverse the stress-related issues in my body. Little things like remembering to breathe and focusing on your breath is a good way to bring yourself into the moment or stopping, taking a moment to take in your surroundings, or acknowledging those who you are in the company of. When you are able to just be, your level of service to those who you are showing up for will increase because your focus is in the present moment.

The process of falling in love with yourself starts with being present, living in the now, recognizing that happiness arises from within, not being dependent on something happening outside of ourselves, and, of course, being okay with telling yourself, "I love you." Try it.

Mind Chatter

Mind chatter is the constant conversation we have in our heads. It's our internal voice rambling on and on. Have you ever stopped and just allowed your mind to go wherever it wants to? One minute, you are thinking about a grocery list. The next, you are in a crazy scenario. I do it all the time. We all do.

Discovering the book and movie *The Secret* was an eye-opening experience for me. For those of you who haven't read the book or seen the movie, do so. The concept of *The Secret* is that the content of our thoughts creates our reality. I began to pay attention to my internal conversations, and I have to say I was surprised at the negativity that went through my mind about myself from the moment I woke up to the moment I went to bed.

Once I became aware of this negative self-talk, I practiced reversing the conversations with positive and uplifting ones. I started small because, once again, we are not conditioned to talk to ourselves kindly and it's uncomfortable at first.

As I continued this practice, I experienced shifts in my daily routine and found that my time became more productive. I was able to get more done in the day, and if I didn't get everything done, I was okay. In the past, I would tear myself down when I didn't meet deadlines or meet expectations. As I began to incorporate the intention of leading with service, I found that the first and most important person I could be of service to was me, simply by changing the conversation I had with myself.

For one week, pay attention to your mind chatter. Write down the conversations you typically have with yourself and see if the content surprises you. I know I was. The following week, begin to converse with yourself with kind, loving, and compassionate thoughts. See the ways you respond and the changes you begin to experience by simply changing your mind chatter.

Your Reality Is a Mirrored Reflection of Your Thoughts.

In today's world, we are inundated with what I like to call the "how tos," that is, the how to get rich quick, how to lose twenty pounds in a week, and how to be a better parent, salesperson, spouse, and so on. All these methods contribute to becoming a better "whoever we want to be." In most cases, this is a recipe for how to become someone that we are not.

We live in a world where information is coming to us on a constant basis. We are glued to our phones, laptops, tablets, and televisions. The problem with the easy access we have to this endless stream of information is that many of us have become obsessed with other people's lives: what they are doing, who they are with, what they are wearing, if they have gained or lost weight, or what their successes and failures are. We have a distorted outlook on what is considered to be attractive, smart, healthy, the right way of doing something versus the wrong way, and good or bad.

Because of this epidemic of comparing ourselves to others, many of us have a plummeting sense of self-worth: how we can match up to an image that the media and we ourselves perceive as being perfect? We think we need to change who we are, and we search for those quick fixes outside of ourselves. We reach for the latest how-to. Our focus has turned to what we can do to become who we are not instead of embracing the essence of who we really are.

Bring awareness to the content of your thoughts. What do you spend most of your time thinking about? What do you want to change about yourself or feel you need to change to become what you have decided you need to be? When your thoughts are focused on that which you don't have or don't want, you begin to create lack, and you draw the exact things you don't want into your reality. Your life becomes a mirror image of your thoughts.

I have experienced this concept firsthand in my personal and professional life. I recently had a year in my sales career when all I would think about was beating my numbers from the year before. I lost sight of my purpose and intention of service and focused on what I didn't want to happen, which in my mind was going backward in production. At the time, I didn't realize that the year I was trying to beat was the year that I solely led from the intention of service. I focused so much on what I didn't want to happen that it became my reality! I worked diligently on my contracts, all the time worrying that something would happen during the contract period that would keep them from closing. Sure enough, one by one, each contract failed. I ended the year defeated and couldn't understand why I failed.

It wasn't until I fully became aware of my purpose—and the power in leading with service—that I was able to see how my attitude, thoughts, and lack of self-love had set me back. It's amazing how quickly things turned around once I was able to redirect my thoughts and intention back to leading with service. It happened almost instantly.

The key is evaluating the content of your thoughts and noting how your reality is mirroring them. When your reality is not what you desire, give up resisting what you don't want and simply change your thoughts. You have to be present. You have to find yourself love, compassion, and understanding. Be mindful of your thoughts, and remove those that no longer serve you.

Determining Your Value

What does it mean to determine your value? Is it what we believe we should gain in return for our time, services, or efforts? That is a part of it. The other part is the value of our experiences. Let's talk first about the value of what we get in return from doing our job. Most salespeople work on either commission or a minimal salary with commission or bonuses. Upon entering the sales world, we decide we are willing to let go of the security of having a regular paycheck because we will obtain the skills, knowledge, and talent to make a living in working as a salesperson. Next, we decide that there is a value on the services that we offer and we will work with those who see the value in what we do.

Now, we have all had many encounters with those who don't see our value, and they want us to discount our services. In real estate sales, we are regularly asked to reduce the agency fee that is charged to market and sell a home or property with the same level of service and end result being expected. I have participated in training specifically on how to deal with clients when this arises. There is also an underlining issue at work here. Think about the first time this happened to you and your reaction.

What happened the next time you went into another sales encounter? After the first time this happened to me, I began to feel insecure about asking for the return that was customary for my time and services. It's kind of funny how it all works. Once I began to feel insecure, it seemed that, in subsequent encounters with potential clients, I was always asked to discount my time and services. Now I see that my thoughts created my reality. For a while, I felt like I was constantly trying to justify my worth to my clients. Some who agreed; others went elsewhere.

We all have moments where we feel like we either have control or lost it. When we are trying to control the outcome, we tend to find ourselves being challenged. For me, this happened when I proclaimed to have control over my worth, my value. On doing so, everything seemed to spin out of control, and I had a hard time asking for what I was worth. When I decided to let go of control, things begin to shift.

This is an important aspect in changing to the mind-set and approach of leading with the intention of service. When I solely led with the intention of service, I was naturally drawn to those who did not question the value of my time and services. I attracted colleagues and clients who not only valued my time and services but expressed gratitude and appreciation for me. I formed more personal relationship with those I was working with, and I know most of those will carry forward because of the bond built during our time together.

The next part of determining our value is through our experiences. It starts with not letting the opinions of others effect what you feel you are worth. When you are in an encounter where your value is in question, understand that you can't control the opinion of others. You can't let those opinions rattle you or make you second-guess yourself. It's a decision that you make to work with them or let them go. When you stand in your power and embrace your value, you will find that you will attract those who see your value and express gratitude for what you bring to the table.

It's a tough world out there, and we are constantly being tested. When you are in love with who you are, you have compassion for yourself, you are able to forgive yourself, and you are able to let go, you stand in the present, confident in who you are and your abilities. This presence will allow you to see when doors open for you and when it is time to close others. It's empowering to know that, by simply falling in love with ourselves, we have the ability to embrace our destiny and release outside influences as simply opinions or a test of our ability to stand within our power.

Giving and Receiving

When you begin to lead with the intention of service in what you do as a salesperson, not only do you discover your purpose, you also align with a powerful universal truth. When you are giving, you are in a state of receiving. When you are genuinely in a place of giving, when you give freely and have no attachments to the outcome and expect nothing in return, you bring forth the energy of receiving, and you will experience the generosity of the universe. Part of the process of looking at what we have to offer is to look within. What can we offer to be a greater contributor to our family, friends, neighbors, communities, and all whom we encounter? What is the one thing we are all searching for, the one thing that we believe will bring us happiness, the one thing that can bring us great joy or great loss? That one thing is love!

Love makes the world go round. We will do many things in the name of love. Being in love is like riding a roller coaster. We experience the great highs when in love and great lows when we fall out of love. How can we experience constant love? How can we avoid the ups and downs in the name of love? It's a process of discovering that love is not outside of us. Love is not something that is received or given away. Love is something that is attainable within us. It's the process of falling in love with you, loving yourself to the point that you don't need love externally. But you can enjoy it when you are in its presence.

This was a huge shift for me. I woke up one day and realized I was placing my happiness in the name of love outside of myself. I was basing my joy, self-worth, and experiences on the ability of others to make me feel loved. What I realized is that everyone experiences love differently. What makes me feel loved is not the same that would make the next person feel loved. I decided I was going to find love within myself, and soon all I thought was missing in my life began to show up. I found compassion for those I'd given the responsibility of meeting my need to feel loved. I found that there was love there. It just wasn't in the form I was expecting.

What does falling in love with you have to do with giving and receiving? There are two parts to this answer. When you begin to love yourself, you begin to give yourself all you need, all you thought was only obtainable outside of yourself. You begin to feel better and lighter, and you see the world from a different perspective. Life doesn't happen to us. Life is what we make it. When you give yourself love, the world will respond, and you will receive love in everything you do.

The second part is that, once you fall in love with you, you begin to lead all you do with love. You project the energy of love externally. Love is the essence of who we are, but we tend to lose that essence through our many experiences. When we discover love within and we begin to radiate love to those we encounter, our realities begin to shift. We live more fully in the natural state of who we truly are meant to be. The process of falling in love with you is a journey. It's letting go of all of our doubts, fears, judgments, perceptions, and hang-ups. It starts within when we give to ourselves and others, and then we will receive in turn.

For me, finding self-love has been a recent discovery, and it's a daily effort to offer genuine love to myself. But I have begun to experience the miracles that self-love offers. I read a book called *Love Yourself Like Your Life Depends On It* by Kamel Ravikant. It's a quick read but an impactful one. Through his own personal journey, he demonstrates the discovery of self-love and the tremendous impact it had on his life. He offers a great self-love exercise that is simple but life changing. He notes that there is power in simplicity, and his message blew me away. I do believe there is power in simplicity. I didn't know how to define it until I read this book. I was able to discover a purpose by going back to the basics. Once again, we all share in this opportunity. Enjoy the process of falling in love with you!

Take a moment now to digest and think about what we have uncovered. Then apply the 4 × 4 Method to fall in love with you.

1. Identify your self-love opportunity. Ask yourself challenge questions:

1. What does falling in love with yourself mean to you?
2. What situations make you feel love for you?
3. What situations make you feel unloved?
4. How would you rate your self-love on a scale from one to ten?

2. Identify the types of obstacles that are in your path in falling in love with you? Please write four examples. This will help identify what needs to be cleared. For example, "I don't like the way I look in the mirror."
   1.
   2.
   3.
   4.

3. Follow these steps to help clear obstacles for finding love for you! Here you are bringing about the change:
   1. Identify your earliest memory that formed your beliefs about self-love. For example, "Loving yourself is boastful."
   2. If your beliefs are positive and self-love-based, praise your experience and honor them. Write it out. If you find your early experiences toward self-love are negative and ego-based, write down how you would have preferred it to be.
   3. Visualize yourself within your positive scenarios, embracing that younger you and wonderful experience of self-love.
   4. Give thanks for the new awareness. Post a note where you will be able to see it to remind you regularly that unconditional love for yourself fills you!

4. State your goal/intention for creating the frequency of self-love. Write the opposite to your list of obstacles here. Now it is time to create! For example, "Loving myself is not boastful but necessary for my well-being and happiness."
   1.
   2.
   3.
   4.

CHAPTER 7

Let Your Light Shine

What we achieve inwardly will change outer reality.

—Plutarch

It's human nature to seek out a fulfilled life. The problem is that we struggle with finding fulfillment because we allow our life events to define who we are. There is a common belief that we are not worthy of happiness or fulfillment. This feeling of unworthiness has no value, but when thoughts that support this belief consume us, we begin to block our truth and purpose from coming forth. The experience of true happiness eludes us.

In this chapter, we will be discussing how you can find your path to happiness and fulfillment by getting back to the basics. In leading with an intention of being of service, you will uncover your truth, passion, and purpose and release the belief of being unworthy. We will discuss these processes through the following concepts:

- Discover Your Truth
- Find Yourself, Find Your Purpose, and Discover Happiness
- The Service Intention
- Light Up the Room

Discover Your Truth

What is truth, and what does it mean to discover our truth? My definition of truth is the experience of discovering yourself for who you really are.

It's about letting go and just allowing yourself to be. Now, you may be thinking that this is much easier said than done. It is a difficult process to let go of our stories. The key is acknowledging that they are just stories, just moments in time. They are not who we are. Releasing yourself from the stories will allow you to simply be. It's a liberating process because, once you have discovered your truth, you begin to see the world with a new lens. You begin to have compassion and understanding for yourself and others on a whole new level.

We have all had different people come in and out of our lives, some leaving an inspiring lasting impression, others leaving a bad taste, and more leaving a deep wound. If we hang on to the bad experiences and miss the good times, as if there are not more of those good times to come, we then begin to build roadblocks for ourselves in discovering our truth. We begin to feel that we are unworthy, and we define ourselves based on our past experiences.

I have been my own worst critic for years. No one has been harder on me than I have. I neglected my intuition that would make relentless attempts to offer me support and guidance, but most of us choose to learn the hard way. I wasn't an exception. The process of discovering my truth came about as I developed an understanding that everything that happens in our world is solely for learning and our growth. Those experiences that push you outside of your comfort zone will leave a lasting impression. The key through those experiences is to have the awareness of the lesson and not to regress to what makes us feel safe or comfortable.

When we resist the lessons that are coming forth, the universe will make other attempts to get our attention. That is why it is so important when something seems to not be going our way. We are to stop and ask ourselves, "What is the lesson I am supposed to learn?"

When the awareness of the lesson is brought forth, whatever you may be experiencing will begin to mend. The key is allowing yourself to stumble and fall, get back up, brush yourself off, pat yourself on the back for trying, and be gentle and kind during both the good and bad times. Trust in life's timing and the fact that certain individuals come in and out of our lives for our personal growth. Each trial and tribulation endured allows us to come out on the other side as a stronger person.

Remember, we too can be an encounter for growth and learning in the lives of others. This is why it is so important to shine our lights and be uplifting to those who need us as part of their learning experience. When you live and work with the intention of service, others are often inspired to find their purpose through service. This is when our individual journeys have a much larger impact than we could have imagined. With this awareness, we no longer feel unworthy or defined by our history. When we serve a purpose, we feel empowered.

We have an obligation to be authentic and true to our nature. This is an idea that I am just starting to be fully acquainted and comfortable with. For most of my life, I lived with the belief that I wasn't good enough and I needed to look and act a certain way to fit in. I was concerned with what others would think or say about me. I have been in situations where my insecurities have been tested, and in many instances, I was left questioning myself.

What we have to understand is that we cannot let the opinion of others stop us from living our truth. We can't change ourselves to fit the mold that others dictate for us. We can't let others stop us from doing what we feel inspired to do because others are oftentimes dealing with their own set of insecurities.

At times, we seek out those who are a reflection of what we would like to be or what we would like to accomplish. We are naturally conditioned to be competitive. It's not uncommon to be confronted with others who may be sabotaging our progress because they see in us what they want to be or do. When you are in the presence of someone who is attempting to sabotage you, find compassion and forgiveness because you can't fall victim to those individuals. Stand in your own authentic power, and make them aware that you are not going to be taken advantage of.

Once the issue is addressed, don't hang onto it. Don't allow it to trip you up and cause you to regress. When faced with someone who is attempting to sabotage or steer you off your path to be rattled, it's not uncommon to become caught up in the "Why me?" When you understand that those attempts are less about you and more about them, you will find it easier to find compassion and forgiveness for them and to continue on your own journey.

Find Yourself, Find Your Purpose, and Discover Happiness

True happiness comes from living with the acceptance that you bring a uniqueness and inspiration by being just you. When you let go of worrying about who you will impress, what others are thinking or saying about you, and what changes you need to make to be a better person, then you have the ability to focus on what you can contribute to those you see on a daily basis. When your intention is to lead from a place of service—and the statistics, numbers, and sales processes are secondary—you will begin to experience true happiness. Your day job becomes a channel for your purpose to shine through. You are able to release the unnecessary stress that is associated with working in a highly competitive industry, you begin to experience the benefits of the universe, and you find a happiness that is not tied to anything external.

The Service Intention

In the sales world, it's all about beating out the competition. What can be done to get to the top? Who is out performing who and being number one? I have learned that, when you become so focused on what everyone else is doing, you begin to lose sight of yourself and what is in the best interest for your clients.

In my early twenties, I worked for a company that raised money for a real estate investment fund. The company was growing quickly and attracted many investors who were interested in participating in the return the fund offered. My boss was a woman in her early sixties who had taken a small mortgage company that did individual construction loans to a company with a registered hundred million-dollar securities offering.

Once the fund went live, she became consumed with beating the company's main competitor. In fact, it became an obsession. She spent thousands of dollars on ineffective advertising. She sent her sales team, me included, to the competitor's workshops so we would know exactly what they were doing and how they were doing it. The company went from being a flourishing enterprise to a company focused on beating out one competitor. The sales manager treated the entire sales team so poorly that they began to leave. I was one of the last to leave, and at the time, I was hurt because I had given so much to this company, and I believed in loyalty. Most of my team members that had left actually went to work for the competition that was the target of my boss.

A year after I left, I got a notice in the mail that the Securities Exchange Commission was investigating my previous boss and sales manager. It turned out that she had created fraudulent loans and was using investor's funds to make the interest payments to maintain the fund. Her attempts to outperform her competition became a fraudulent business that lost millions of dollars, most of which were monies invested by retirees and people's life savings. The end result was the company went completely under, monies of innocent people were lost, and my previous boss went from owning a thriving business and living very comfortably to losing everything. She was convicted of the charges brought against her and served prison time.

Now, this is an extreme example, but if this person had not been so intent on taking down her competitor, if she had instead focused that same time and energy to be of service to her clients by offering a productive investment through the real estate fund, the outcome for the company and her would have been completely different.

The power of living with a service intention benefits all those involved. It removes the need to be competitive. It creates an urge to seek out any and all that you have an opportunity to be of service to, including those that may be your competition. If you take the skills, tools, and knowledge you obtain from your training as a salesperson and lead with the intention of service, those processes become enjoyable, and you experience your purpose in your day-to-day activities. For me, it was my opportunity to shine my light and become something much bigger than just being a real estate agent.

Light Up the Room

Over the years, I've had the opportunity to hear Lisa Nichols, a transformational speaker and founder of the company Motivating the Masses, speak on a couple occasions. The first time I heard Lisa, I was sitting in the front row, and she captivated me from the moment she took the stage. When Lisa enters the room, this energy just fills the space, and she completely lights up the room. She is a perfect example of what it means to lead with the intention of service.

Lisa Nichols has built a multimillion-dollar business helping others transform their lives. Her journey is inspirational. I admire her because I want to command the presence that Lisa does by just being Lisa. She isn't boastful, she isn't arrogant, she isn't demanding, and she isn't pushy. She is pleasant, she is uplifting, and she opens a door for you to look inside yourself to see what needs attention or reevaluation. I believe that part of what makes her so captivating is her genuine desire to be that light to those who may be in search of what she has to offer. I know she was the light I needed at one point, and she inspired me to try on a new experience, one that was uncomfortable for me but also necessary for my personal growth.

We all have our own unique avenue to be the light for others. I think the impact I have experienced by many lights like Lisa Nichols, who came into my life at the exact moment I needed them the most, has inspired me to be the light that others may need. We all have this same opportunity. Rather than waiting around for life to show us what we need to do, it's time to acknowledge this opportunity to take action and shine our light. When you are happy, on purpose, and in service to others, your light will naturally shine, and others will feel your presence in a positive way. They will be drawn to you, they will want to be around you because you make them feel good and uplifted, they will value your efforts, and they will tell everyone they know about you.

When you are genuinely leading with the mind-set to apply your tools, skills, and knowledge to benefit those you have the opportunity to be of service to, you will experience joy in your everyday practices, even the more mundane ones.

My mundane practice was prospecting. Prospecting is a common practice in sales and was probably the least favorite part of my job. I dreaded the time I spent making those calls. I didn't want to be that person who interrupted someone's day, that annoying salesperson who called at the wrong time. The day I had the encounter with a sales coach that shifted my perspective, I was fortunately able to realize that I was making those calls to find the next person to be of service to. It was that simple. Now I actually enjoy picking up the phone, and those I call are more receptive. I attract clients that are drawn to my service intention energetically.

We don't realize the power inherent in our feelings or thoughts. The responses I got on the phones when I was dreading and forcing myself to make those phone calls were usually cold and uninterested. When I make those calls with the intention of service, I found the responses much more receptive, almost as people have been waiting for me to call.

I was amazed by the fact that I had the ability to change my outcome by simply changing the content of my thoughts and intention. Not only did this experience allow me to find myself and happiness, it began to attract the things into my life that I was striving for, and they showed up effortlessly. This is a simple but profound process. It starts with acknowledging the value we each bring to the table.

Next, we strip down everything and start from a basic concept of leading with service. We follow it up with rearranging our priorities with the knowledge that, when we make service to others our number-one priority, the universe will take care of the rest. We have the opportunity to cultivate these practices every day. Discovering purpose through these daily rituals is a liberating process. Be that person who makes a difference in someone's day. As you shine your internal light, your world will begin to change, so let your light shine!

Take a moment now to digest and think about what we have uncovered. Then apply the 4 × 4 Method and let your light shine.

1. Identify your ability to let your light shine. Ask yourself challenge questions:
   1. What does letting your light shine mean to you?
   2. What situations make you feel you are living with a shining light?
   3. What situations make you feel you are not living with a shining light?
   4. How would you rate that you are living with your shining light on a scale from one to ten?

2. Identify what types of obstacles are in your path to fully being able to shine your light. Please write four examples. This will help identify what needs to be cleared. For example, "Could I even have a positive impact on others by shining my light?"
    1.
    2.
    3.
    4.

3. Follow these steps to help clear obstacles for you to live with your light shining. Here you are bringing about the change:
    1. Identify your earliest memory that formed about your light shining. For example, "Not everyone is able to live with the ability to shine his or her light."
    2. If your beliefs are positive in relation to living with your light shining, praise your experience and honor them. Write it out. If you find your early experiences toward your light shining are negative and ego-based, write down how you would have preferred it to be.
    3. Visualize yourself within your positive scenarios, embracing that younger you and wonderful experience of living with your life shining.
    4. Give thanks for the new awareness. Post a note where you will be able to see it to remind you regularly that you are filled with abundant and fulfilling with light shining-based intentions!

4. State your goal/intention for creating the frequency of leading with your light shining. Write the opposite to your list of obstacles here. Now it is time to create! For example, "I am grateful for the growth opportunities that allow me to live by shining my light."
    1.
    2.
    3.
    4.

CHAPTER 8

Spread the Word! Spread the Love!

Spread love everywhere you go. Let no one ever
come to you without leaving happier.

—Mother Teresa

As we make lifestyle changes and learn new skills, we are releasing old habits to make room for the new. In doing so, we can be the inspiration for others in the hope they too can make changes to allow them to experience the happiness that arises when we practice self-love and lead a life of service.

In this chapter, we will learn also how we can apply the multiplier effect to share our inspiration with others. We will be covering the following topics and ways they apply to spreading the word and love:

- Surrender the Need to Be Competitive
- Pay It Forward
- It's Contagious in the Best Way

Surrender the Need to Be Competitive

What kind of place would the world be if the concept of competition didn't exist? How would removing the need to be competitive change our interactions with one another? Competition is food for the ego. That drive removes us from our true essence. I find it funny at times when I reflect back on my career in sales and how I ended up doing what I do. I have never been an overly competitive person. I don't like to see others feel bad, so when I ended up working in one of the most highly competitive industries, you somewhat have to laugh about it, right? I have the outlook that there is enough to go around for everyone. We live in an abundant universe, and coming from a place of competitiveness contradicts the nature of that which surrounds us.

When you surrender the need to be competitive by allowing service to lead the way, you align with the abundance of the universe. Competition is a need to be in control or possibly demonstrate lack of control. When we are competing to control the situation or outcome, we are actually blocking ourselves from what we are truly meant to accomplish. We are sending a subconscious message to the universe that there isn't enough to go around, so we must fight for what we need. If the content of our thoughts become our reality and we are leading from a place of competition, then we are setting ourselves up to attract undesirable outcomes. In the short term, we may gain those small wins, but is there any depth to those wins?

The emotions that come into play when living in a competitive state are jealousy, fear, anger, self-doubt, and worry. Jealousy is typically felt when someone has something we would like to have or he or she has accomplished something we would like to accomplish. Fear is a product of not having something we would like to have, not accomplishing something we would like to accomplish, or not being able to live up to an idealized version of who we think we should be. We become angry when things don't seem to go the way we need or want them to go. We begin to doubt our abilities and ourselves, and in turn, we create worry about what the future may hold. Do you see the emotional turmoil that can be produced when we are in a place of competition?

When we begin to compare who we are as not being adequate or good enough in relation to others, we step right out of a position of authentic power, and we are no longer aligned with our truth. The solution is to make the decision to surrender the need to be competitive, embrace that there truly is more than enough to go around, and release the need to compare ourselves to others.

When you lead with the intention of service, competition naturally begins to fall away. You focus on the unique gifts and abilities you possess to contribute in your world. The world opens its doors to opportunities for you when you start to view your purpose from the standpoint of finding those who need your help. You meet new people who have an impact on you, or you have an impact on them.

By surrendering our need to be competitive, we begin to release the limited beliefs we formed by needing to be, do, or have something we are not. The basis of finding purpose is in the now. Being of service is an expression of freedom and allows expansion of your world. When you lead with the intention of service and release the need to be competitive, you are naturally incorporating love into your daily practices. As you lead from the place of love, you are spreading love to all those you encounter.

Pay It Forward

You never know when you will have an impact on someone else's day. I believe that is why I love the concept of paying it forward. What does it mean to pay it forward? To pay it forward is the process of doing an unexpected act of kindness for someone and, in turn, inspiring that person to do an unexpected act of kindness for someone else. Could you imagine what life would be like if we were all going around doing unexpected acts of kindness? It would be a much happier place. They say the quickest way to pull yourself out of a slump or low point is by doing something kind for someone else or volunteering to help those in need. We have an opportunity to practice paying it forward on a daily basis: in our work, while running errands, and at home. This is the beauty of leading with the intention of service. In everything we do, we have an opportunity to make a difference in someone else's day.

Think about a time when you were just going about your routines and someone paid you an unexpected compliment that made you smile. Did it make a difference in your day? Were you inspired to share that moment with others, or did you pay it forward by paying someone else a compliment because you knew that it made you feel good and you wanted someone else to share in that experience? We don't always know when someone needs to hear just what we have to say in that moment or when something we do for someone fills him or her up in a time of need.

In my opinion, it is not an accident that the things we need show up when they do. It is synchronicity. I can think of many times that I needed something and I happened to cross paths with someone who offered what I needed in that moment.

I was recently on a trip and had lunch with a new friend of mine. It was one of those days when, not only was it cloudy outside, I felt like I had a cloud right over my head. I was feeling unloved, left out, tired, and emotional. As I sat with this new friend, I told her a little bit about what I was experiencing and how it was coming to the surface on that particular day. She shared with me some profound advice about our experiences being solely a matter of perception and we have the power to change that perception at any time.

After we finished lunch, I went back to the conference I was attending, and that cloud that had been hovering over me lifted, the feelings of being left out shifted, and my day completely transformed based on that advice I was given over a quick lunch with a new friend. She took the time to listen to me and share with me. This act of kindness changed my entire day.

Later that night, I was at dinner with another friend who shared with me probably one of the biggest compliments I have ever received regarding the support I had offered her in starting a new business. I had no idea that I had made that impact on her, and I was grateful for her sharing it with me. At the time the advice was given, I didn't realize she was in the midst of the decision process regarding her business. She told me—because of my support—she made the decision to go ahead. You never know when you will have an impact on someone else's day, week, month, year, or life. Be that light that shines on someone who in turn will be inspired to shine his or her light on another.

It's Contagious in the Best Way

When you read, hear, or discover something that resonates within you and gives you an aha moment, it's a sign that you have just read, heard, or discovered something that resonates with the essence of who you are beyond this physical world. When I was able to shed the doubts and expectations that I placed on myself and I discovered my job was solely to help others, it resonated with me on many levels. I was able to release the pressure, competition requirements, and stress. I was left with a feeling of excitement. First, my purpose was in the present and wasn't as unattainable as I had expected it to be. Second, I began to truly love what I do. Third, I had to tell everyone I knew about it so they too could experience it for themselves!

It was contagious in the best way. It's impossible to make such a discovery that shifts our worldview without sharing it. I feel we are obligated to share with others ways in which they too can experience happiness, abundance, and love.

We are all vessels of love, and the brighter we shine, the more magnetic we become, and others want to know what our secret is. I believe this is why we are so drawn to those who have experienced success. Rather than feeling the need to be competitive with them, celebrate those successes and accomplishments, and learn from them to begin to draw in similar experiences. Once you have achieved your success and accomplishments, be the light to others who are now looking to you for inspiration and guidance. They say, if you want to change your outcome in your life, surround yourself with those who have paved the way for you, that is, those who have taken the risks to open the doors for themselves and others.

If you come across a door that has not been opened, look at it as an opportunity to discover something that could change the world. We have so many great examples of those who have led fearlessly into the unknown, only to make discoveries that were game changers. We all share in the same opportunity. We are all unique and possess unique gifts that are of value. The problem is that we don't see ourselves as valuable because we are too busy comparing ourselves to those we want to be like. Instead of comparing, let yourself be inspired by them.

The opportunity to share our discoveries is an expansion of the benefits we experience. It's the basis of leading with service. It's the service of sharing our experiences to inspire others to make the same discoveries we have made. It's a snowball effect because, once you share it, they will share it. Then the next will share it, and the snowball gets bigger and bigger.

There is enough to go around for everyone, and we all have the opportunity to truly experience abundance by aligning with the generous universe. Begin this process by allowing yourself to just be, to look at those whom you work with as those who you can be of service to, and to share your secret with others.

The simplicity of it is truly amazing. But it doesn't surprise me that it really isn't as complex as it is expected to be. We are conditioned to think that, if something is worthwhile, it must be difficult to obtain. It is actually the opposite. It merely takes awareness to begin to experience these profound shifts. This concept can be applied in all facets of life. In this case, we are applying it to the sales world and the many men and women of the sales world who can channel their daily activities to be of service and change the world.

Spread the word and love by being the messenger to those searching for what you have to offer. We all have been blessed with unique gifts that are inspirational. Don't keep them to yourself.

Take a moment now to digest and think about what we have uncovered. Then apply the 4 × 4 Method to spread the word and love.

1. Identify how you will spread the word and love. Ask yourself the challenge questions:
    1. What does spreading the word and spreading the love mean to you?
    2. What situations make you feel you are able to spread the word and love?
    3. What situations make you feel you are not able to spread the word and love?
    4. How would you rate your ability to spread the word and love on a scale from one to ten?

2. Identify what types of obstacles are in your path to be able to spread the word and love. Please write four examples. This will help identify what needs to be cleared. For example, "I don't believe I have anything to offer to share or to be inspirational."
    1.
    2.

    3.

    4.

3. Follow these steps to help clear obstacles for you to ultimately spread the word and love. Here you are bringing about the change:
    1. Identify your earliest memory that formed your beliefs about having a story to share. For example, "You can't have it all."
    2. If your beliefs are positive and balance-based, praise your experience and honor them. Write it out. If you find your early experiences toward having a story to share are negative and ego-based, write how you would have preferred it to be.
    3. Visualize yourself as a vessel of light sharing your story and embracing that younger and wonderful experience of having an inspirational and fulfilled life.
    4. Give thanks for the new awareness. Post a note where you will be able to see it to remind you regularly that you are living an inspirational life!

4. State your goal/intention for creating the frequency of leading an inspirational and fulfilled life. Write the opposite to your list of obstacles here. Now it is time to create! For example, "I am grateful for my life story and my ability to spread the word and love to inspire others."
    1.
    2.
    3.
    4.

CHAPTER 9

What's Next

We keep moving forward, opening new doors,
and doing new things, because we are curious and
curiosity keeps leading us down new paths.

—Walt Disney

Upon learning a new outlook, the next step is to begin to implement the newly learned processes in order to experience change. Change is never easy, especially when it forces us to leave our comfort zone. What will it take to get you to make the changes to adapt service into your everyday life, fulfill your purpose, and experience happiness and abundance? When you think about the new life you are about to embark on, it's easy to daydream about all you will do to make it happen. Think about New Year's Day when you are listing your resolutions for the year, and as you are writing them down, you already feel the sense of accomplishment, the motivation for the new activities you will be bringing into your routine.

But as each day passes, we usually settle back into our old routines where comfort resides. Why is it so hard to adopt positive changes, especially when those changes will provide you with the life you desire? In this chapter, we will discuss the answer to that question and introduce tools that can be used to implement these new discoveries that will transform your life. We will break it down by discussing the following concepts and processes:

- When You Cross Paths with Resistance

- Starting Now and Not Tomorrow
- The Power of Visualizing
- Finding Freedom Now and Not When
- The Action Plan

When You Cross Paths with Resistance

Resistance is the roadblock that keeps you from taking the next step and following through. It is the uneasy feeling that comes up when we are about to try something new or different. It is that little voice in our heads that creates doubt in our ability to accomplish what you are setting out to do. We have all come face-to-face with resistance at one time or another. I can think of many times when resistance crept in and took over, stalling any progress I was making or about to make. In *The War of Art* by Steven Pressfield, he explains that we have two lives, one life that we live and the unlived life within us. Between the two lives stands resistance. What does your unlived life look like?

You know when resistance has entered the room because it is good friends with fear, doubt, and worry. Have you ever wanted to do something but the thought of it terrified you? Well then, you have met resistance. Most of us have faced resistance many times. We fall victim to the "what ifs." What if the business fails? What if no one likes my idea? What if my idea has already been taken? What if we run out of money? What if no one shows up? What if no one likes what I have to offer? Do any of those what-ifs sound familiar?

A year ago, I was faced with resistance when I had an opportunity to write and submit a book proposal. As you know, my passion is writing. I did all the setup around the writing process, but one thing I didn't start was the actual writing. I was halfway through the time I had in order to complete the proposal, and every day, I came face-to-face with resistance. Then I had an amazing experience where the universe made it very clear that I needed to push through my resistance. It made it clear that, even though I felt unsure about what I was going to write, whom I was writing for, and how to do it, I needed to do it anyway. The challenge was met, and I started. I loved it and enjoyed the time I would spend writing.

Every now and then, resistance would show up to try to trip me up and make me feel insecure, but I just kept going. Once I was on the other side of it and I accomplished my goal of completing the proposal and submitting it by the deadline, I understood the lesson I had just learned. Regardless of what happens, resistance will show up, and even though it makes you feel uneasy, insecure, and afraid, do it anyway. I can promise from personal experience that, once you cross the finish line, the feeling of accomplishment outweighs the speed bumps endured along the way. We have the ability to create our realities. It's not an easy process because it takes standing up to resistance. It takes faith when you feel your faith account is depleted, and it takes courage. Nothing in life that is worth it is easy, so they say.

As you begin to explore the process of leading with service, allow yourself to be guided by your intuition. New doors will open, new opportunities will present themselves, and at times, resistance will be present. Push through it the first time, and it gets easier from there. They say the first time in everything is always the hardest, but after the icebreaker, it's game on!

Starting Now and Not Tomorrow

A little trick I have learned in conquering resistance is to not spend much time thinking about getting started. When you think too much about the actual process of starting anything, you can just as easily talk yourself out of it as you talked yourself into. There is something about saying to yourself, "I will start tomorrow." Then tomorrow comes, and once again, you will start tomorrow. I am the queen of starting things tomorrow. I can't tell you how many workout routines or new projects at home or work I was going to start. And it was always going to be tomorrow. Initially, you feel reassured because, at the time, you feel like you really will start tomorrow. But tomorrow comes, and something happens. The time allocated to start the project is gone.

The key is developing your action plan, and once you have the action plan ready to go, there is no better time to start than now. Procrastination and resistance are best friends, and they love it when they get their way. They meet up at the end of the day and share stories of how many hopes and dreams they put off that day. Don't give them anything to talk about. Don't open yourself to any excuses that will keep you from implementing your action plan.

The Power of Visualizing

Visualization is a practice in which you see the outcome of what you desire in your mind. Some professional athletes use the practice of visualization to enhance their performance during a game or in a competition. I became intrigued with the concept of visualization when I discovered *The Secret* and I began to study the effects that support the idea that our thoughts do create our reality. When you are visualizing something, your mind cannot decipher what is reality and what is a thought. In your mind, what you are visualizing is present and occurring, and in turn, your external world begins to reflect the content of your thoughts.

Throughout my travels and in the many workshops and seminars I have attended, I've noticed that a common practice shared by individuals whom I admire for their presence and the way they light up the room is visualization. They all tell their stories of success found and ways they visualized it before they actualized it. I found this fascinating, and I've begun a daily practice of meditation and visualization. This practice has brought me great clarity and peace of mind as I make my own journey.

One of my favorite stories about the power of visualization is Jim Carrey's story. Before he was famous, he would drive to Mulholland Drive, park his car, and visualize himself getting the things he wanted, acting parts and success. At one point, he wrote himself a check for ten million dollars and dated it for three years out. Right before the three years expired, he was offered a part in the movie *Dumb and Dumber,* and he was paid ten millions dollars. He shared this story with Oprah, and he said it's not just about visualizing. It's also about taking action. He didn't set limits on himself, that is, how he was going to actualize his dreams. He knew it was going to happen. The process of visualization includes feeling the emotions associated with what you are visualizing, incorporating your senses, and, most important, not getting in your own way. Enjoy the process, let the "how" go, and take action.

Finding Freedom Now and Not When

Everyone is seeking freedom, and we work hard to achieve it. What does freedom look like to you? For me, freedom is having the security that would allow me to do the things I love and enjoy, be with those I love, and live peacefully. The actualization of freedom is commonly expressed in achieving financial success that will allow you to spend your time as you chose. How many times have you told yourself that, when some event important to you occurs, at some point in the future, you will finally know freedom?

I know I have told myself that countless times and felt like I was constantly chasing freedom and not experiencing it in the present moment. I began to ponder on this. Why couldn't I have freedom now? Why did I have to wait for something to happen in order to truly feel free? I discovered that, by having the mind-set that freedom is in the present moment, the things I sought for in order to achieve freedom in my life began to show up much quicker.

Isn't it funny how that works? When I began to lead my business solely with the intention of service and when I discovered that doing so allowed me to live my purpose and experience happiness, joy, and abundance, I realized I was free. Freedom isn't a product of having to go down the checklist and make sure it's all marked off before you can experience it. I no longer chase the idea of being free because I've changed my perspective. I am free. Now we spend so much time telling ourselves that we can achieve peace, happiness, freedom, and love when something happens in the future, but all we really have is the present moment. So why not experience them all now?

The Action Plan

The action plan is the outline of the steps you will take to make things happen. This is a fun process because it is limitless. The only limitations are what we place on ourselves. It's time to be fearless and just do it! What is your action going to be? How will you begin to lead with the intention of service?

1. Change our mind-set. We need to be aware of our thoughts, and if we are not thinking in the fashion that supports our mission, we need to bid those thoughts farewell and welcome in the new set of thoughts that are supportive. This process starts with you.

2. Create a routine of self-love. Loving yourself is believing in yourself. It's very important. This is a confidence builder, an internal confidence builder! Remember, when coming from a place of internal confidence, your confidence always remains intact. It never leaves your side.

3. Identify who will be the beneficiary of your service. You have tools, skills, and knowledge that will guide you in the right direction. This is a fun process because there is this internal light that you will feel when you start thinking about who you will be of service to. Most likely, this is the same group of people you are already working amongst. They haven't changed, but you have, and you see them quite differently. Before I made this transition, I had the mind-set of having to talk to so many people per day in order to reach my monthly or annual production goals. Everyone was just a contact to add to the production formula. The life-changing shift occurred when I changed, not the contacts around me.

4. Announce to the universe that you are now a service agent. This is a matter of just showing up every day with the intention to be of service. Service is the leader in all you do. When you are starting a new project or taking on a new client, you evaluate it from how you are serving. Now, I get excited before a new client even walks through the door for his or her appointment. I'm thrilled that I am getting ready to meet someone that I can be of service to. As we are discussing his or her needs, I am thinking about the various ways I can make his or her life easier, and I assure him or her that my number-one priority to him or her is service. Everyone likes to know that he or she is being looked out for. No one likes to be looked at as a paycheck opportunity. When you are working in sales and working primarily on commission basis, you typically don't get paid until the deal is done, but no one wants to feel as if you are only working with him or her to get paid. When you lead with the intention of service and bring a fresh energy into every deal, you have the opportunity

to work, and the paycheck becomes the reward. The universe is very generous when you are aligned with the higher frequency of an intention such as service. The beauty of it is that the stress, worry, and unpredictability of being a salesperson falls away because you have aligned with abundance and know that, as a service agent, you are living your purpose.

5. Continue to search for ways to be of service to others in all aspects of your life. Not only is this a business or work concept, it's also a personal one. Service comes in all shapes and sizes. Be of service to yourself by adopting positive activities such as daily meditation and self-love. Be the light to your family and colleagues, and inspire them so they too want to lead with service. The more service agents we have, the better place the world is going to be.

Remember, there is enough to go around for everyone. Let's unite, release the need to compete with one another, and discover all the ways we can show up to be of service. Let's begin to live out our life purpose now and not when. Let's have tremendous amounts of love for ourselves, a knowing that love comes from within and not outside of us. Let's lead all we do with love and intention of service. While we are at it, let's change the world together by being fearless and unreasonable service agents! Why not? Sounds fun!

Take a moment now to digest and think about what we have uncovered. Then apply the 4 × 4 Method in becoming a service agent.

1. Identify how you will become a service agent. Ask yourself challenge questions:
    1. What does becoming a service agent mean to you?
    2. What situations make you feel you are able to be a service agent?
    3. What situations make you feel you are not able to be a service agent?
    4. How would you rate your ability to be a service agent on a scale from one to ten?

2. Identify what types of obstacles are in your path to be able to become a service agent. Please write four examples. This will help identify what needs to be cleared. For example, "I am afraid of change and

don't know if I can implement the processes needed to make the shift."

1.

2.

3.

4.

3. Follow these steps to help clear obstacles for you to ultimately become a service agent. Here you are bringing about the change:

    1. Identify your earliest memory that formed your beliefs about living a purpose through being a service agent. For example, "You can't have it all."
    2. If your beliefs are positive and balance-based, praise your experience and honor them. Write it out. If you find your early experiences toward living a purpose to share are negative and ego-based, write down how you would have preferred it to be.
    3. Visualize yourself as a service agent and embracing that younger you and wonderful experience of having an inspirational and a fulfilled life.
    4. Give thanks for the new awareness. Post a note where you will be able to see it to remind you regularly that you are living a purposeful life!

4. State your goal/intention for creating the frequency of being a service agent. Write the opposite to your list of obstacles here. Now it is time to create! For example, "I am grateful for my life purpose in showing up as a service agent."

    1.

    2.

    3.

    4.

www.ingramcontent.com/pod-product-compliance
Lightning Source LLC
Chambersburg PA
CBHW022105170526
45157CB00004B/1485